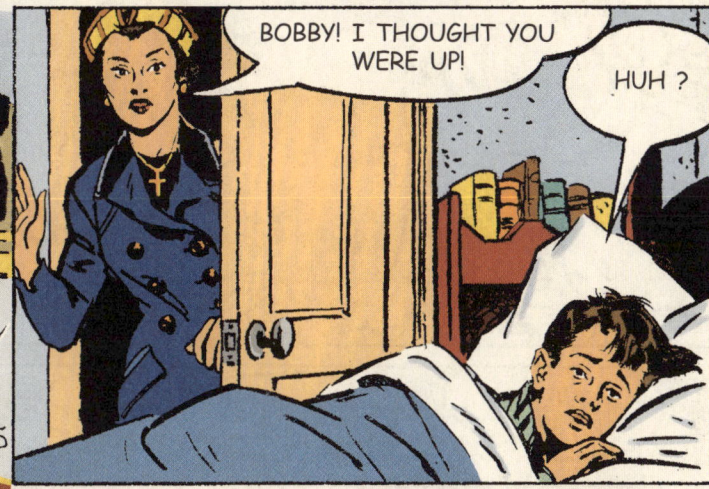

KNOW YOUR MASS

CHAPTER ONE: ALL DRESSED UP

HELLO. I'M YOUR PARISH PRIEST, AND THIS IS THE SACRISTY.

OVER HERE WE KEEP THE VESTMENTS OR CLOTHES THAT THE PRIEST WEARS AT MASS.

THIS IS AN AMICE. IT IS MADE OUT OF WHITE LINEN.

ORIGINALLY IT WAS A COVERING FOR THE HEAD. IT IS STILL WORN THAT WAY BY SOME RELIGIOUS—LIKE THIS. TODAY MOST PRIESTS WEAR IT ABOUT THE NECK AND SHOULDERS.

HERE IS AN ALB. IT'S LIKE A BIG, LOOSE DRESS. IT IS ALSO MADE OF LINEN.

KNOW YOUR MASS

CHAPTER TWO: TWO MASSES IN ONE

BEFORE YOU STUDY THE MASS PART BY PART YOU SHOULD UNDERSTAND THE MASS AS A WHOLE. THE WHOLE MASS IS DIVIDED INTO TWO PARTS:

1. **THE MASS OF THE CATECHUMENS**
   FOR: CATHOLICS AND THOSE WHO ARE PREPARING TO BECOME CATHOLICS.
   TO: OFFER PRAYER AND RECEIVE INSTRUCTION.

2. **THE MASS OF THE FAITHFUL**
   FOR: CATHOLICS ONLY.
   TO: RE-OFFER THE SACRIFICE OF THE CROSS, AND RECEIVE OUR LORD IN HOLY COMMUNION.

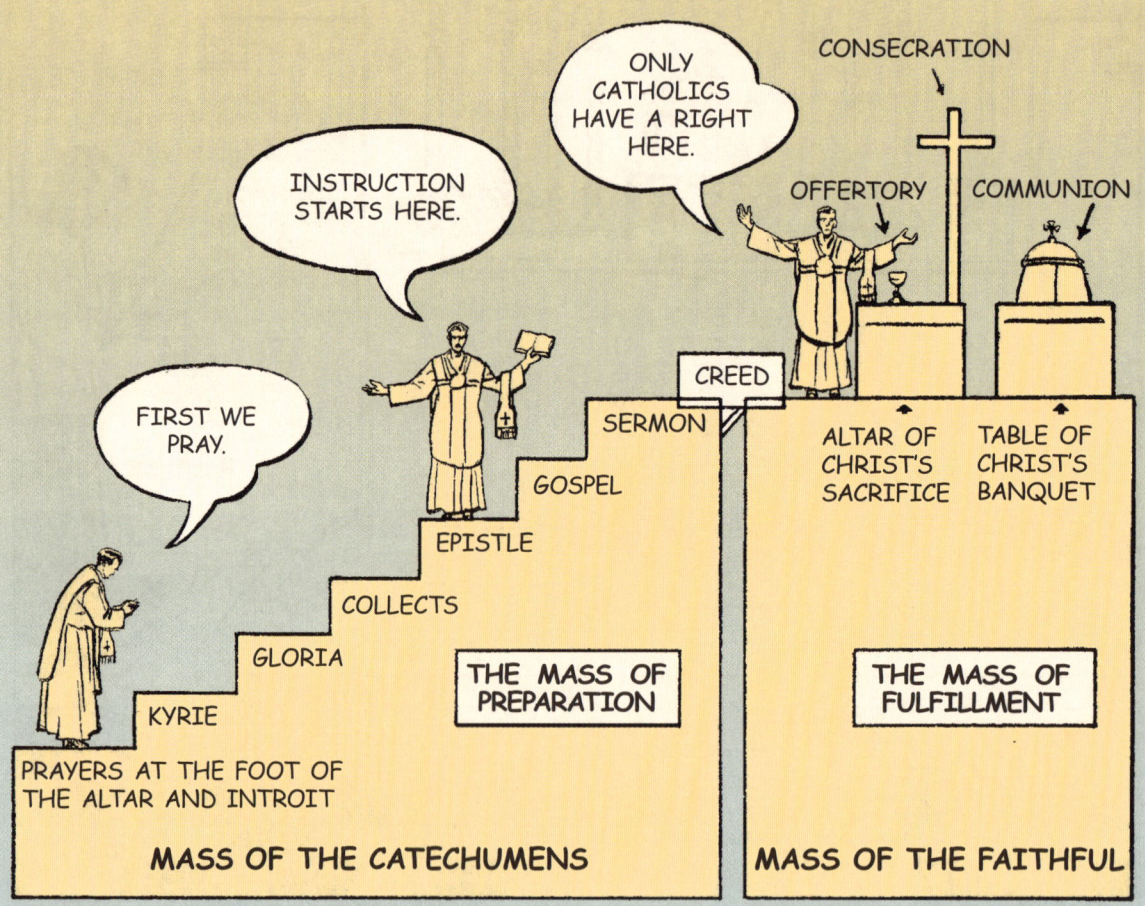

AFTER YOU'VE STUDIED THE REST OF THIS BOOK, COME BACK AND STUDY THESE PICTURES AGAIN.

NOW LOOK AT THE MASS OF THE CATECHUMENS BY ITSELF. IN THE FIRST HALF WE LIFT OURSELVES TO GOD BY PRAYER (WITH THE HELP OF HIS GRACE, OF COURSE). IN THE SECOND HALF HE LIFTS US TO HIMSELF BY INSTRUCTING US (AND HIS GRACE HELPS US LISTEN).

THE FIRST HALF, THEREFORE, IS LIKE AN ORDINARY STAIRWAY. THE SECOND HALF, LIKE A MOVING OR MECHANICAL STAIRWAY.

KNOW YOUR MASS CHAPTER THREE: GETTING READY

HERE IS HOW THE MASS BEGINS. WATCH THE PRIEST CAREFULLY.

YOU SHOULD BE IN YOUR SEAT AND WAITING <u>BEFORE</u> THE PRIEST LEAVES THE SACRISTY.

← YOU STAND NOW.

YOU GENUFLECTED BEFORE YOU ENTERED YOUR PEW. THE PRIEST GENUFLECTS NOW.

IN GENU-FLECTING TO GOD YOU BEND YOUR <u>RIGHT</u> KNEE TO THE GROUND.

TAKING THE CORPORAL OUT OF THE BURSE, THE PRIEST SPREADS IT OVER THE PLACE WHERE THE ALTAR STONE IS.

THE BLESSED EUCHARIST MUST ALWAYS REST ON THE CORPORAL.

THE PRIEST NOW OPENS THE MASS BOOK (OR MISSAL) AT THE PROPER PLACE.

THE MISSAL RESTS ON A SPECIAL STAND AND HAS RIBBONS TO MARK THE PLACES.

THEN THE PRIEST RETURNS TO THE FOOT OF THE ALTAR AND GENUFLECTS.

NOW YOU KNEEL.

IN THE NAME OF THE FATHER...

THE MASS BEGINS WITH THE SIGN OF THE CROSS. YOU SHOULD MAKE THE SIGN WITH THE PRIEST. NOTICE HOW IT IS MADE.

...AND OF THE SON...

WHAT DOES THE SIGN OF THE CROSS TELL US?

THE <u>SIGN</u> TELLS US THAT GOD BECAME MAN AND DIED FOR US.

THE <u>WORDS</u> TELL US THAT THERE ARE THREE PERSONS IN ONE GOD.

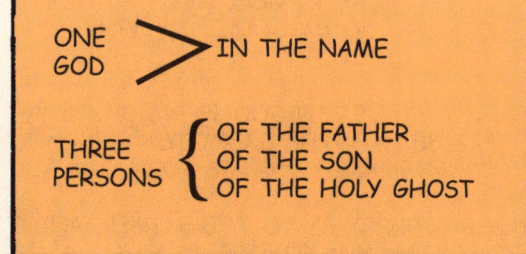

THE PRIEST AND SERVER RECITE PSALM 42.

THIS PSALM WAS WRITTEN BY KING DAVID TO EXPRESS HOW MUCH HE WANTED TO GO BEFORE THE ALTAR OF GOD.

PRIEST: GIVE JUDGMENT FOR ME, O GOD, AND DECIDE MY CAUSE AGAINST AN UNHOLY PEOPLE; FROM UNJUST AND DECEITFUL MEN DELIVER ME.

SERVER: FOR THOU, O GOD, ART MY STRENGTH. WHY HAST THOU FORSAKEN ME? AND WHY DO I GO ABOUT IN SADNESS, WHILE THE ENEMY AFFLICTS ME?

PRIEST: SEND FORTH THY LIGHT AND THY TRUTH; THEY HAVE LED ME AND BROUGHT ME TO THY HOLY HILL AND THY DWELLING PLACE.

SERVER: AND I WILL GO TO THE ALTAR OF GOD, TO GOD, THE JOY OF MY YOUTH.

PRIEST: I SHALL YET PRAISE THEE ON THE HARP, O GOD, MY GOD. WHY ART THOU SORROWFUL, MY SOUL, AND WHY DOST THOU TROUBLE ME?

SERVER: TRUST IN GOD, FOR I SHALL YET PRAISE HIM, THE SALVATION OF MY COUNTENANCE AND MY GOD.

PRIEST: GLORY BE TO THE FATHER, AND TO THE SON, AND TO THE HOLY GHOST.

IT SHOULD EXPRESS OUR JOY IN BEING ABLE TO ATTEND MASS.

LONG AGO THIS PSALM USED TO BE RECITED BY THE PRIEST AS A PREPARATION BEFORE HE CAME TO THE ALTAR. NOW IT IS SAID AT MASS ITSELF, BUT IT IS STILL A PREPARATION.

SERVER: AS IT WAS IN THE BEGINNING, IS NOW, AND EVER SHALL BE, WORLD WITHOUT END. AMEN.

PRIEST: I WILL GO TO THE ALTAR OF GOD.

SERVER: TO GOD, THE JOY OF MY YOUTH.

IN THE MASS JESUS IS GOING TO BE OFFERED UP FOR OUR SINS. THEREFORE, WE FIRST TELL HIM WE ARE SORRY FOR THEM.

BECAUSE MARY MAGDALENE WAS TRULY SORRY FOR HER SINS, JESUS NOT ONLY FORGAVE HER, BUT LOVED HER VERY MUCH.

IF WE ARE TRULY SORRY FOR OUR SINS JESUS WILL LOVE US TOO.

SERVER: I CONFESS TO ALMIGHTY GOD, TO BLESSED MARY EVER VIRGIN, TO BLESSED MICHAEL THE ARCHANGEL, TO BLESSED JOHN THE BAPTIST, TO THE HOLY APOSTLES PETER AND PAUL, TO ALL THE SAINTS, AND TO YOU, FATHER, THAT I HAVE SINNED EXCEEDINGLY IN THOUGHT, WORD, AND DEED, THROUGH MY FAULT, THROUGH MY FAULT, THROUGH MY MOST GRIEVOUS FAULT. THEREFORE, I BESEECH BLESSED MARY EVER VIRGIN, BLESSED MICHAEL THE ARCHANGEL, BLESSED JOHN THE BAPTIST, THE HOLY APOSTLES PETER AND PAUL, ALL THE SAINTS, AND YOU, FATHER, TO PRAY TO THE LORD OUR GOD FOR ME.

PRIEST: MAY ALMIGHTY GOD HAVE MERCY UPON YOU, FORGIVE YOU YOUR SINS, AND BRING YOU TO LIFE EVERLASTING.

SERVER: AMEN.

THEN IT IS THE PEOPLE'S TURN TO TELL GOD THEY ARE SORRY FOR THEIR SINS.

YOU SHOULD SAY THE CONFITEOR WITH THE SERVER. MEMORIZE IT IF YOU DON'T ALREADY KNOW IT.

MAY THE ALMIGHTY AND MERCIFUL GOD GRANT US PARDON, ABSOLUTION, AND FULL REMISSION OF OUR SINS.

AMEN.

WHEN WE GO TO MASS WE ARE LIKE THE GOOD THIEF WHO HUNG AT JESUS' RIGHT UPON THE CROSS.

HE ASKED JESUS, AND JESUS FORGAVE HIM ALL HIS SINS.

THOU WILT TURN, O GOD, AND BRING US TO LIFE.

AND THY PEOPLE SHALL REJOICE IN THEE.

THE PRAYERS AT THE FOOT OF THE ALTAR ARE THE "PRIVATE" PRAYERS OF THE PRIEST AND THE PEOPLE PREPARING THEM FOR THEIR PART IN THE MASS.

IF THE MASS IS A HIGH MASS, THE CHOIR WILL HAVE BEEN SINGING THE "PUBLIC" PREPARATION DURING THIS TIME.

THIS PUBLIC PREPARATION IS CALLED THE "INTROIT."

PRIEST: SHOW US, O LORD, THY MERCY.
SERVER: AND GRANT US THY SALVATION.
PRIEST: O LORD, HEAR MY PRAYER.
SERVER: AND LET MY CRY COME UNTO THEE.
PRIEST: THE LORD BE WITH YOU.
SERVER: AND WITH THY SPIRIT.

LET US PRAY. TAKE FROM US OUR SINS, O LORD, THAT WE MAY ENTER WITH PURE MINDS INTO THE HOLY OF HOLIES. THROUGH CHRIST OUR LORD. AMEN.

WE BESEECH THEE, O LORD, BY THE MERITS OF THY SAINTS WHOSE RELICS LIE HERE, AND OF ALL THE SAINTS, DEIGN IN THY MERCY TO PARDON ME ALL MY SINS. AMEN.

BEFORE RECITING THE INTROIT HIMSELF, THE PRIEST GOES UP TO THE ALTAR, ONCE MORE ASKS PARDON FOR HIS SINS, AND KISSES THE ALTAR STONE.

ALTAR STONE LIES IN THE CENTER OF THE ALTAR.

THE STONE IS BLEST BY THE BISHOP.

RELICS OF MARTYRS ARE KEPT SEALED IN THE STONE.

THE ALTAR, AND ESPECIALLY THE ALTAR STONE, REPRESENTS THE BODY OF CHRIST. HENCE IT IS KISSED REVERENTLY.

HAVING PROCEEDED TO THE EPISTLE SIDE OF THE ALTAR, THE PRIEST STANDS BEFORE THE MISSAL AND BLESSES HIMSELF. THE PRIEST NOW READS THE INTROIT, THE FIRST VARIABLE PART OF THE MASS. AT HIGH MASS THE INTROIT IS ALSO SUNG BY THE CHOIR.

NOTICE THAT THE PRIEST BOWS HIS HEAD WHENEVER HE SAYS: "GLORY BE TO THE FATHER, ETC."

VERY OFTEN THE INTROIT IS TAKEN FROM PART OF THE PSALMS. LONG AGO THE WHOLE PSALM WAS SUNG IN A PROCESSION TO THE ALTAR.

NOW ONLY PART OF THE PSALM OR SOME OTHER SHORT VERSE IS USED. BUT IT STILL SHOWS THE PROPER NATURE OF THE DAY'S PARTICULAR FEAST. HENCE IT IS CALLED PART OF "THE PROPER" OF THE MASS AND CHANGES WITH EACH FEAST.

IN THIS BOOK THE PROPER PRAYERS ARE ALL TAKEN FROM THE MASS FOR TRINITY SUNDAY. YOUR MISSAL HAS THE PROPER PRAYERS FOR EVERY DAY.

KNOW YOUR MASS

CHAPTER FOUR: TALKING TO GOD

WE ARE NOW READY TO TAKE THE FIRST STEP IN THE PART OF THE MASS OF THE CATECHUMENS WHERE WE TALK TO GOD.

THE FIRST STEP IS THE KYRIE. ALL THE OTHER MASS PRAYERS ARE IN LATIN. THIS PRAYER IS IN GREEK, WHICH IS ONE OF THE OLDEST LANGUAGES IN WHICH MASS HAS BEEN OFFERED.

PRIEST: LORD, HAVE MERCY ON US. → FATHER
SERVER: CHRIST, HAVE MERCY ON US.
PRIEST: CHRIST, HAVE MERCY ON US. → SON
SERVER: CHRIST, HAVE MERCY ON US.
PRIEST: LORD, HAVE MERCY ON US.
SERVER: LORD, HAVE MERCY ON US. → HOLY SPIRIT
PRIEST: LORD, HAVE MERCY ON US.

WE ASK EACH PERSON OF THE TRINITY THREE TIMES TO FORGIVE US OUR SINS.

IT IS SAID ONLY ON JOYFUL FEASTS.

AND ON EARTH PEACE TO MEN OF GOOD WILL. WE PRAISE THEE. WE BLESS THEE. WE ADORE THEE. WE GLORIFY THEE. WE GIVE THEE THANKS FOR THY GREAT GLORY. O LORD GOD, HEAVENLY KING, GOD THE FATHER ALMIGHTY. } **FATHER**

O LORD JESUS CHRIST, THE ONLY-BEGOTTEN SON; LORD GOD, LAMB OF GOD, SON OF THE FATHER, WHO TAKEST AWAY THE SINS OF THE WORLD, HAVE MERCY ON US. WHO TAKEST AWAY THE SINS OF THE WORLD, RECEIVE OUR PRAYER. WHO SITTEST AT THE RIGHT HAND OF THE FATHER, HAVE MERCY ON US. FOR THOU ALONE ART HOLY. THOU ALONE ART THE LORD. THOU ALONE, O JESUS CHRIST, ART MOST HIGH. } **SON**

THE GLORIA WITH ITS ADORATION AND THANKSGIVING IS ALSO ADDRESSED TO THE THREE PERSONS OF THE TRINITY.

TOGETHER WITH THE HOLY GHOST, IN THE GLORY OF GOD THE FATHER. AMEN. } **HOLY SPIRIT**

AFTER THE GLORIA THE PRIEST KISSES THE CENTER OF THE ALTAR. THEN TURNING TO THE CONGREGATION, HE GREETS THE PEOPLE.

HE DOES THIS WHENEVER HE WANTS TO CALL THEIR ATTENTION TO A VERY SPECIAL PART OF THE MASS.

HAVING RETURNED TO THE EPISTLE SIDE THE PRIEST BOWS TOWARD THE CRUCIFIX AND SAYS: "LET US PRAY."

THE SPECIAL ACTION THIS TIME IS THE COLLECTS—OR ORATIONS—THE PRAYERS OF PETITION.

THE PRIEST PRAYS WITH ARMS OUTSTRETCHED AS MOSES PRAYED WHEN HE WANTED GOD TO HELP THE ISRAELITES IN BATTLE.

IN EVERY COLLECT WE ASK GOD THE FATHER FOR SOME FAVOR THROUGH THE SON IN UNION WITH THE THREE DIVINE PERSONS AGAIN!

SOME MASSES HAVE ONE COLLECT. OTHERS HAVE SEVERAL. THE COLLECTS CHANGE WITH EACH MASS.

KNOW YOUR MASS CHAPTER FIVE: LISTENING TO GOD

NOW THAT WE HAVE TALKED TO GOD, HE SPEAKS TO US. NOTICE HOW THE TRINITY IS REPRESENTED HERE TOO.

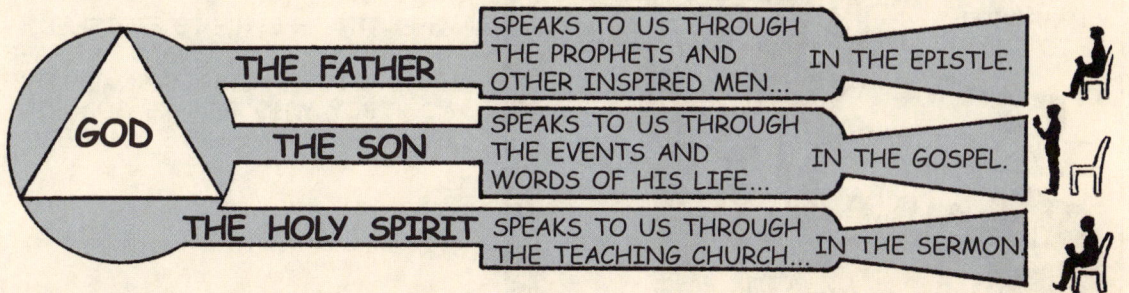

THE FATHER SPEAKS TO US THROUGH THE PROPHETS AND OTHER INSPIRED MEN... IN THE EPISTLE.

THE SON SPEAKS TO US THROUGH THE EVENTS AND WORDS OF HIS LIFE... IN THE GOSPEL.

THE HOLY SPIRIT SPEAKS TO US THROUGH THE TEACHING CHURCH... IN THE SERMON.

"LESSON FROM THE EPISTLE OF THE BLESSED APOSTLE PAUL TO THE ROMANS."

THE EPISTLE IS READ RIGHT AFTER THE COLLECTS.

YOU MAY SIT DOWN HERE.

OH, THE DEPTH OF THE RICHES OF THE WISDOM AND OF THE KNOWLEDGE OF GOD! HOW INCOMPREHENSIBLE ARE HIS JUDGMENTS AND HOW UNSEARCHABLE HIS WAYS! FOR WHO HAS KNOWN THE MIND OF THE LORD, OR WHO HAS BEEN HIS COUNSELLOR? OR WHO HAS FIRST GIVEN TO HIM, THAT RECOMPENSE SHOULD BE MADE HIM? FOR OF HIM, AND BY HIM, AND IN HIM, ARE ALL THINGS. TO HIM BE GLORY FOR EVER. AMEN.

MANY EPISTLES ARE TAKEN FROM THE LETTERS OF SAINT PAUL, BUT OTHERS ARE CHOSEN FROM THE ACTS OF THE APOSTLES, THE APOCALYPSE OF SAINT JOHN, THE LETTERS OF OTHER APOSTLES, OR THE OLD TESTAMENT.

THE EPISTLE IS CHOSEN TO FIT THE FEAST OR OCCASION.

ALTHOUGH IT IS POSSIBLE TO HAVE MORE THAN ONE EPISTLE AT A MASS, ONLY A FEW MASSES DURING THE YEAR HAVE MORE THAN ONE.

WHEN THE EPISTLE IS FINISHED, THE PRIEST, BY EXTENDING HIS LEFT HAND ON THE ALTAR, SIGNALS THE ALTAR BOY, WHO THANKS GOD FOR THE LESSONS WE HAVE LEARNED.

ALLELUIA, ALLELUIA. BLESSED ART THOU, O LORD THE GOD OF OUR FATHERS, AND WORTHY OF PRAISE FOR EVER. ALLELUIA.

AS THE SERVER COMES TO GET THE MISSAL THE PRIEST READS SEVERAL SHORT PRAYERS.

THESE PRAYERS EXPRESS OUR JOY AT HAVING CHRIST TEACH US. HENCE AT HIGH MASS THESE PRAYERS ARE SUNG.

LIKE THE EPISTLE, THESE PRAYERS ALSO CHANGE WITH THE FEAST.

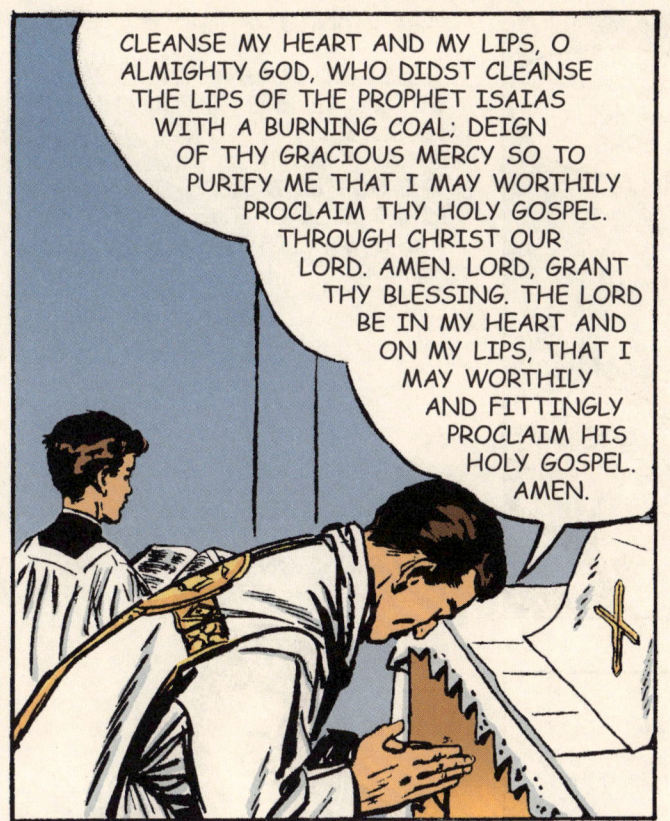

THE PRAYERS ARE:

THE GRADUAL: CALLED GRADUAL BECAUSE THE OLD CANTORS USED TO STAND ON THE ALTAR STEPS WHEN THEY SANG.

THE ALLELUIA: A VERY SHORT SONG OF PRAISE. "ALLELUIA" IS A HEBREW WORD MEANING "PRAISE GOD."

THE TRACT: A LONGER, LESS JOYFUL PRAYER WHICH TAKES THE PLACE OF THE ALLELUIA DURING SAD OR PENITENTIAL TIMES.

ON CERTAIN FEASTS A LONG POEM IS ADDED TO THE ALLELUIA OR TRACT. THIS IS CALLED **THE SEQUENCE**.

AFTER THESE PRAYERS THE MISSAL IS TAKEN TO THE OTHER SIDE OF THE ALTAR, AND THE PRIEST SAYS A SPECIAL PRAYER ASKING GOD TO HELP HIM READ THE GOSPEL WORTHILY.

YOU STAND FOR THE GOSPEL.

WE STAND DURING THE GOSPEL OUT OF REVERENCE FOR CHRIST'S WORDS.

THE GOSPEL IS READ ON THE RIGHT SIDE OF THE ALTAR. THE RIGHT SIDE IS THE PLACE OF HONOR.

TO BEGIN THE GOSPEL THE PRIEST SIGNS HIMSELF WITH THE CROSS ON HIS FOREHEAD, LIPS, AND HEART. YOU DO IT TOO:

THE GOSPEL IS READ WITH FOLDED HANDS. FOLD YOURS TOO.

RIGHT WAY

WRONG WAY

WRONG WAY

THE GOSPEL IS ALWAYS FROM ONE OF THE FOUR BIOGRAPHERS OF CHRIST: MATTHEW, MARK, LUKE, OR JOHN. IT TOO CHANGES WITH THE FEAST.

AT THE END, THE PRIEST KISSES THE BOOK OUT OF REVERENCE.

ON SUNDAYS THE PRIEST USUALLY GIVES A SERMON OR INSTRUCTION AFTER THE GOSPEL.

THE SERMON IS A REAL PART OF THE MASS. IT IS AN IMPORTANT WAY IN WHICH GOD SPEAKS TO US.

BEFORE THE SERMON THE PRIEST USUALLY READS THE GOSPEL AGAIN IN OUR OWN LANGUAGE.

SIT DOWN NOW.

DURING THE SERMON YOU SHOULD BE AS QUIET AS YOU CAN AND PAY VERY CLOSE ATTENTION.

KNOW YOUR MASS

CHAPTER SIX: THE PASSWORD

I BELIEVE IN ONE GOD, THE FATHER ALMIGHTY, MAKER OF HEAVEN AND EARTH, AND OF ALL THINGS VISIBLE AND INVISIBLE. AND IN ONE LORD JESUS CHRIST, THE ONLY-BEGOTTEN SON OF GOD, BORN OF THE FATHER BEFORE ALL AGES. GOD OF GOD, LIGHT OF LIGHT, TRUE GOD OF TRUE GOD; BEGOTTEN, NOT MADE; OF ONE BEING WITH THE FATHER, BY WHOM ALL THINGS WERE MADE. WHO FOR US MEN, AND FOR OUR SALVATION CAME DOWN FROM HEAVEN.

AND WAS MADE FLESH BY THE HOLY GHOST OF THE VIRGIN MARY: AND WAS MADE MAN.

ON SUNDAYS AND IMPORTANT FEAST DAYS THE PRIEST RECITES THE CREED AS SOON AS HE RETURNS TO THE ALTAR. IT IS THE NICENE CREED.

THE CREED EXPRESSES THE CHIEF THINGS A CATHOLIC MUST BELIEVE. IT IS OUR ACT OF FAITH IN THE THINGS WE HAVE LEARNED IN THE EPISTLE, GOSPEL, AND SERMON.

HENCE IT IS AN EXCELLENT PREPARATION FOR THE MASS OF THE FAITHFUL. IT IS LIKE A PASSWORD LETTING US INTO THE GREAT MYSTERY OF THE MASS.

THE MASS OF THE FAITHFUL MEANS THE MASS OF THOSE WHO BELIEVE.

BELIEVE WHAT?

BELIEVE EVERYTHING IN THE CREED.

AT THE WORDS WHICH REMIND US OF THE MOMENT WHEN JESUS BECAME MAN WE GENUFLECT IN ADORATION. (AT HIGH MASS, WHEN THE CREED IS SUNG, WE KNEEL.)

JESUS BECAME MAN AT THE MOMENT WHEN MARY TOLD THE ANGEL THAT SHE WAS WILLING TO BECOME THE MOTHER OF GOD.

HE WAS ALSO CRUCIFIED FOR US, SUFFERED UNDER PONTIUS PILATE, AND WAS BURIED. AND ON THE THIRD DAY HE ROSE AGAIN, ACCORDING TO THE SCRIPTURES; AND ASCENDED INTO HEAVEN, AND SITTETH AT THE RIGHT HAND OF THE FATHER: AND HE SHALL COME AGAIN WITH GLORY TO JUDGE THE LIVING AND THE DEAD: AND OF HIS KINGDOM THERE SHALL BE NO END. AND I BELIEVE IN THE HOLY GHOST, THE LORD AND GIVER OF LIFE, WHO PROCEEDETH FROM THE FATHER AND THE SON: WHO TOGETHER WITH THE FATHER AND THE SON IS ADORED AND GLORIFIED: WHO SPOKE BY THE PROPHETS. AND IN ONE, HOLY, CATHOLIC, APOSTOLIC CHURCH. I CONFESS ONE BAPTISM FOR THE REMISSION OF SINS. AND I LOOK FOR THE RESURRECTION OF THE DEAD, AND THE LIFE OF THE WORLD TO COME. AMEN.

NOTICE HOW THE CREED IS DIVIDED INTO WHAT WE BELIEVE CONCERNING EACH OF THE THREE PERSONS OF THE TRINITY—WITH THE DOCTRINES OF THE CHURCH, BAPTISM, RESURRECTION OF THE DEAD, AND ETERNAL LIFE ADDED AT THE END.

WITH THE CLOSE OF THE CREED (OR IMMEDIATELY AFTER THE GOSPEL IN MASSES WHERE THERE IS NO CREED) WE HAVE CROSSED THE BRIDGE THAT LEADS FROM THE MASS OF THE CATECHUMENS TO THE MASS OF THE FAITHFUL.

THE LORD BE WITH YOU.

AND WITH THY SPIRIT.

THE MASS OF THE FAITHFUL BEGINS BY THE PRIEST'S CALLING THE PEOPLE TO ATTENTION IN THE USUAL WAY.

YOU MAY SIT DOWN NOW.

IN THE EARLY DAYS OF THE CHURCH ALL PUBLIC SINNERS AND THOSE WHO WERE NOT CATHOLICS HAD TO LEAVE THE CHURCH AT THIS POINT.

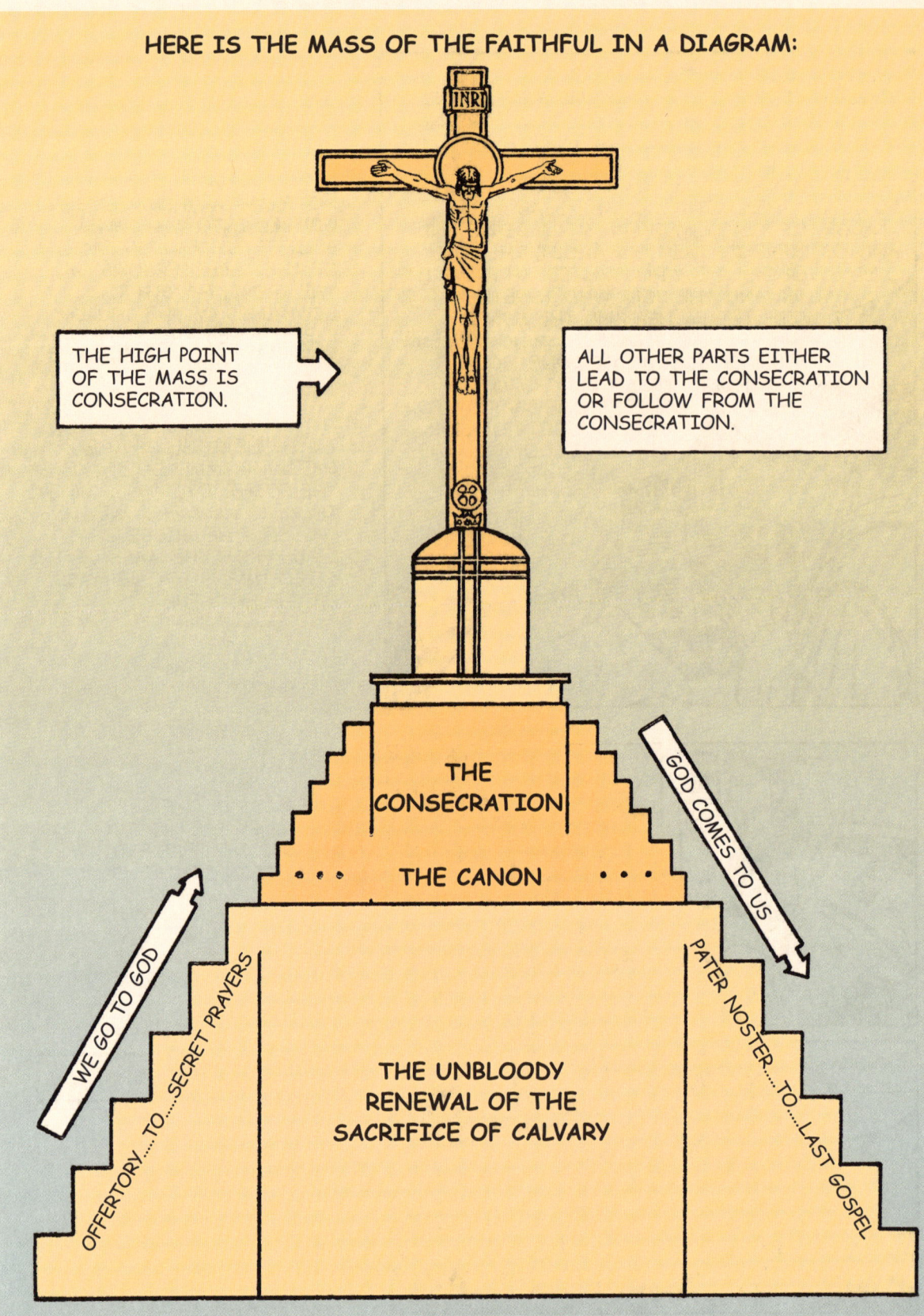

KNOW YOUR MASS

CHAPTER SEVEN: WE BRING GIFTS

FROM THE OFFERTORY TO THE SECRET PRAYERS WE PREPARE FOR THE GREAT SACRIFICE BY

1. PREPARING THE OFFERINGS
2. CONFESSING OUR UNWORTHINESS
3. ASKING FOR HELP

AS THE PRIEST GOES UP THESE STEPS →

YOU GO UP THESE STEPS. →

Steps (bottom to top):
- OFFERTORY VERSE
- OFFERING OF OF THE BREAD
- MIXING WATER WITH THE WINE
- OFFERING OF THE WINE
- PRAYER FOR HUMILITY
- PRAYER FOR THE HOLY SPIRIT
- LAVABO
- PRAYER TO THE HOLY TRINITY
- ORATE FRATRES
- SECRETS

WHAT THE PRIEST DOES ➤

WHAT THE PEOPLE SHOULD DO ➤

- OFFERTORY COLLECTION
- MAKE ACTS OF CONTRITION
- ASK GOD FOR HELP

YEARS AGO THE OFFERTORY BEGAN WITH A PROCESSION DURING WHICH A SPECIAL PSALM WAS SUNG AS GIFTS WERE BROUGHT TO THE ALTAR.

TODAY WE NO LONGER HAVE THE PROCESSION, SO THE PRIEST READS ONLY A SHORT PRAYER OR VERSE OF THE PSALM. THIS IS CALLED THE OFFERTORY VERSE.

THE OFFERTORY VERSE CHANGES WITH THE FEAST. IT IS SUNG BY THE CHOIR AT HIGH MASS.

IN MANY CHURCHES THE BELL IS RUNG WHEN THE PRIEST UNCOVERS THE CHALICE TO REMIND THE PEOPLE THAT A MOST IMPORTANT PART OF THE MASS IS BEGINNING.

PUTTING THE CHALICE ASIDE, THE PRIEST FIRST OFFERS THE BREAD.

BREAD SYMBOLIZES ALL OF US WHO WILL BE UNITED IN CHRIST THROUGH THE MASS.

JUST AS

| MANY GRAINS OF WHEAT ... | ARE UNITED IN | ... ONE PIECE OF BREAD. |

SO

| MANY DIFFERENT PEOPLE ... | THROUGH CHRIST'S LOVE, ARE UNITED IN | ...ONE CHURCH. |

BREAD IS ALSO A SYMBOL OF CHRIST.

BREAD = NOURISHMENT = LIFE

CHRIST = EUCHARIST = SPIRITUAL LIFE

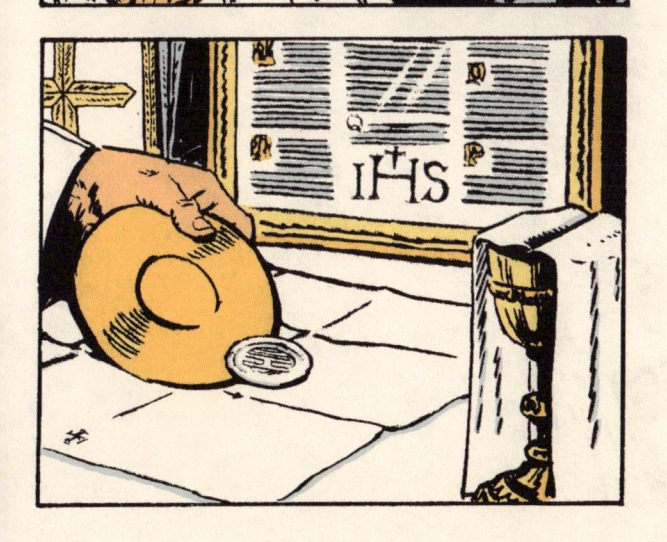

ACCEPT, O HOLY FATHER, ALMIGHTY AND ETERNAL GOD, THIS SPOTLESS HOST, WHICH I, THY UNWORTHY SERVANT, OFFER UNTO THEE, MY LIVING AND TRUE GOD, TO ATONE FOR MY NUMBERLESS SINS, OFFENSES, AND NEGLIGENCES; ON BEHALF OF ALL HERE PRESENT AND LIKEWISE FOR ALL FAITHFUL CHRISTIANS LIVING AND DEAD, THAT IT MAY PROFIT ME AND THEM AS A MEANS OF SALVATION UNTO LIFE EVERLASTING. AMEN.

WHEN WE OFFER THE HOST WITH THE PRIEST, WE LOOK FORWARD TO OUR OFFERING OF JESUS CHRIST, BECAUSE THE BREAD WILL BECOME THE BODY OF CHRIST AT THE CONSECRATION.

WHEN THE PRIEST IS GOING TO CONSECRATE HOSTS FOR THE PEOPLE (IF THERE ARE NOT ENOUGH ALREADY CONSECRATED IN THE TABERNACLE) THE CIBORIUM WITH THE HOSTS IS KEPT ON THE CORPORAL. THE CIBORIUM'S COVER IS KEPT ON EXCEPT
1) WHEN THE PRIEST IS OFFERING THE HOST, AND
2) WHEN THE PRIEST IS CONSECRATING THE HOST.
THE PRIEST NOW OFFERS BOTH THE HOST ON THE PATEN AND THE HOSTS IN THE CIBORIUM AS ONE.

HAVING OFFERED THE HOST, THE PRIEST PUTS THE PATEN ASIDE AND TAKES UP THE CHALICE, CLEANING IT WITH THE PURIFICATOR, THEN HE PUTS WINE INTO THE CHALICE AND ADDS A DROP OR TWO OF WATER.

THE WINE STANDS FOR CHRIST. (IT WILL REALLY BECOME THE BLOOD OF CHRIST AT THE CONSECRATION.)

> O GOD, WHO HAST ESTABLISHED THE NATURE OF MAN IN WONDROUS DIGNITY AND EVEN MORE WONDROUSLY HAST RENEWED IT, GRANT THAT...

THE WATER STANDS FOR US. (WE SHALL BE LOST IN THE BLOOD OF CHRIST AT THE CONSECRATION, JUST AS THE WATER IS LOST IN THE WINE NOW.)

WE ARE THUS UNITED TO CHRIST. (WE "PARTAKE OF HIS DIVINITY.")

AND SO WE ARE OFFERED UP WITH CHRIST IN THE MASS.

> ...THROUGH THE MYSTERY OF THIS WATER AND WINE, WE MAY BE MADE PARTAKERS OF HIS DIVINITY, WHO HAS DEIGNED TO BECOME PARTAKER OF OUR HUMANITY, JESUS CHRIST, THY SON, OUR LORD, WHO LIVETH AND REIGNETH WITH THEE IN THE UNITY OF THE HOLY GHOST, GOD, WORLD WITHOUT END. AMEN.

WHEN GOD THE FATHER RECEIVES THE OFFERING OF HIS SON IN THE MASS, HE RECEIVES US TOO. HE FORGIVES US OUR SINS, OUR WEAKNESSES, AND OUR FAULTS BECAUSE HE LOVES CHRIST SO MUCH, AND WE ARE WITH CHRIST.

"WE OFFER UNTO THEE, O LORD, THE CHALICE OF SALVATION, HUMBLY BEGGING OF THY MERCY THAT IT MAY ASCEND BEFORE THY DIVINE MAJESTY WITH A PLEASING FRAGRANCE, FOR OUR SALVATION AND THAT OF ALL THE WORLD."

JUST AS HE OFFERED THE BREAD, SO THE PRIEST OFFERS THE WINE.

THE OFFERTORY IS ONE OF THE IMPORTANT PARTS OF THE MASS.

IF YOU MISS IT YOU SHOULD ATTEND ANOTHER MASS TO FULFILL YOUR OBLIGATION OF HEARING MASS ON SUNDAYS OR HOLY DAYS OF OBLIGATION.

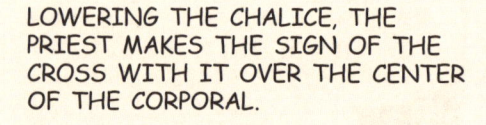

LOWERING THE CHALICE, THE PRIEST MAKES THE SIGN OF THE CROSS WITH IT OVER THE CENTER OF THE CORPORAL.

THEN HE PUTS THE PALL ON TOP OF THE CHALICE.

THE CHALICE IS KEPT COVERED WITH THE PALL SO THAT NOTHING CAN FALL INTO IT BY ACCIDENT.

> IN A HUMBLE SPIRIT AND A CONTRITE HEART, MAY WE BE ACCEPTED BY THEE, O LORD, AND MAY OUR SACRIFICE SO BE OFFERED IN THY SIGHT THIS DAY AS TO PLEASE THEE, O LORD GOD.

HAVING SAID THE PRAYERS OF THE OFFERING, THE PRIEST NOW PRAYS TO GOD TO PURIFY HIM:

1. HE PRAYS FOR HUMILITY AND CONTRITION, WHICH ARE NECESSARY TO PURIFY US FROM PAST SINS.
2. HE ASKS GOD TO BLESS OUR OFFERING SO IT TOO WILL BE PURIFIED.
3. HE WASHES HIS HANDS AS A SYMBOL OF PURITY.

> COME, THOU SANCTIFIER, ALMIGHTY AND ETERNAL GOD,...

> ...AND BLESS THIS SACRIFICE PREPARED FOR THE GLORY OF THY HOLY NAME.

DURING THESE PRAYERS WE SHOULD ASK GOD TO HELP US PAY ATTENTION AND TO CLEANSE OUR MINDS OF EVERYTHING THAT WOULD TAKE US AWAY FROM CHRIST.

"I WILL WASH MY HANDS AMONG THE INNOCENT, AND WILL WALK AROUND THY ALTAR, O GOD, TO HEAR THE VOICE OF THY PRAISE AND TO TELL ALL THY WONDROUS DEEDS. O LORD, I LOVE THE BEAUTY OF THY HOUSE, AND THE PLACE WHERE THY GLORY DWELLS. DESTROY NOT MY SOUL WITH THE IMPIOUS, O GOD, NOR MY LIFE WITH MEN OF BLOOD..."

AT SOLEMN HIGH MASS THE ALTAR IS INCENSED BEFORE THE PRIEST WASHES HIS HANDS.

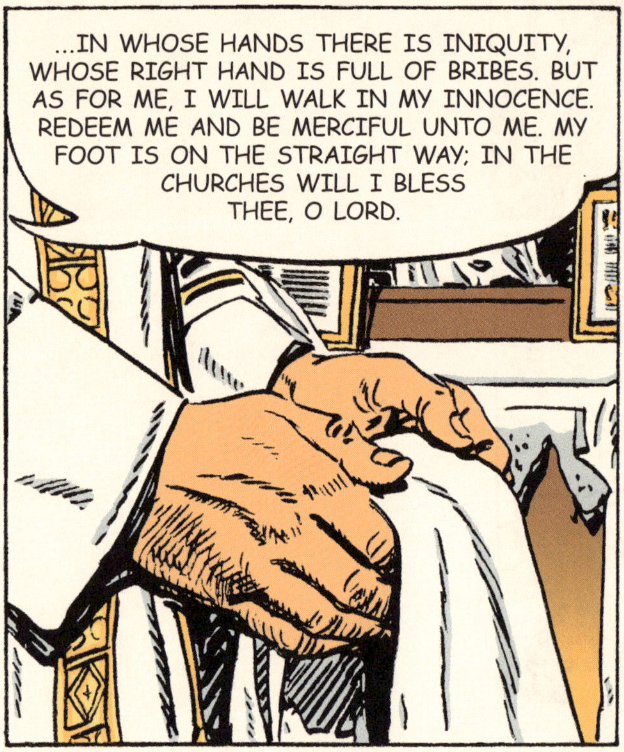

"...IN WHOSE HANDS THERE IS INIQUITY, WHOSE RIGHT HAND IS FULL OF BRIBES. BUT AS FOR ME, I WILL WALK IN MY INNOCENCE. REDEEM ME AND BE MERCIFUL UNTO ME. MY FOOT IS ON THE STRAIGHT WAY; IN THE CHURCHES WILL I BLESS THEE, O LORD."

WASHING ONE'S HANDS IS AN ANCIENT SYMBOL FOR PURIFYING ONE'S SOUL.

IN OLDEN DAYS IT WAS NECESSARY AFTER HANDLING THE DIFFERENT GIFTS WHICH PEOPLE BROUGHT UP TO THE ALTAR.

THE PRAYER SAID BY THE PRIEST AS HE WASHES HIS HANDS IS TAKEN FROM THE BOOK OF PSALMS.

HANDING BACK THE LAVABO CLOTH TO THE SERVER THE PRIEST BOWS AND RECITES THE GLORY BE...

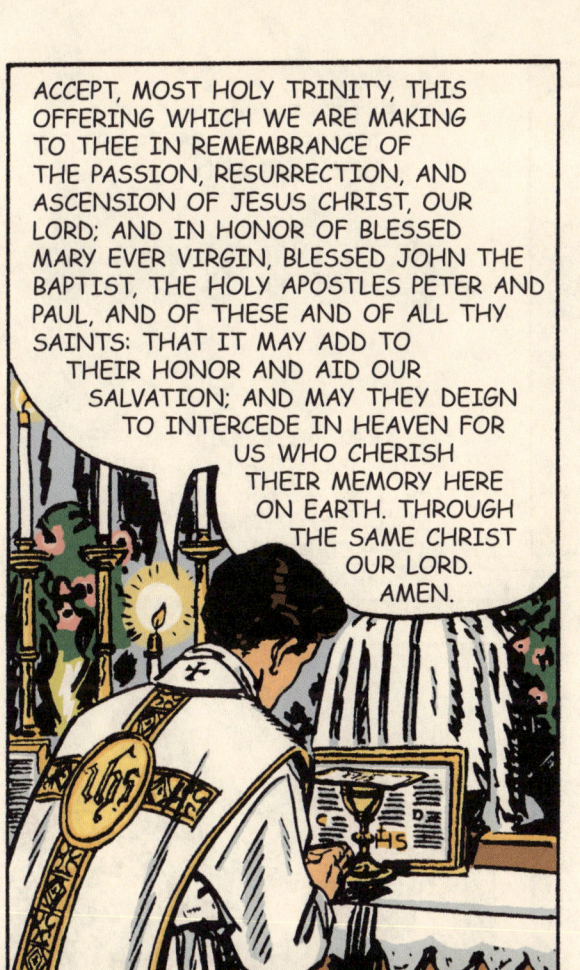

"ACCEPT, MOST HOLY TRINITY, THIS OFFERING WHICH WE ARE MAKING TO THEE IN REMEMBRANCE OF THE PASSION, RESURRECTION, AND ASCENSION OF JESUS CHRIST, OUR LORD; AND IN HONOR OF BLESSED MARY EVER VIRGIN, BLESSED JOHN THE BAPTIST, THE HOLY APOSTLES PETER AND PAUL, AND OF THESE AND OF ALL THY SAINTS: THAT IT MAY ADD TO THEIR HONOR AND AID OUR SALVATION; AND MAY THEY DEIGN TO INTERCEDE IN HEAVEN FOR US WHO CHERISH THEIR MEMORY HERE ON EARTH. THROUGH THE SAME CHRIST OUR LORD. AMEN."

THE THIRD STEP UP TO THE CANON CONSISTS OF THREE PRAYERS IN WHICH WE ASK GOD FOR HELP TO OFFER THE SACRIFICE WORTHILY.

WHILE THE PRIEST IS SAYING THE FIRST OF THESE PRAYERS, THINK OF HOW WE JOIN CHRIST IN THE MASS BOTH AS THE ONE WHO OFFERS THE MASS AND AS THE ONE WHO IS OFFERED IN THE MASS.

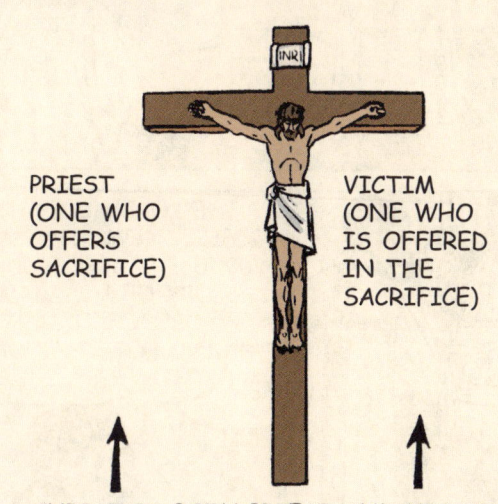

PRIEST (ONE WHO OFFERS SACRIFICE)

VICTIM (ONE WHO IS OFFERED IN THE SACRIFICE)

CHRIST IS BOTH PRIEST AND VICTIM.

SACRAMENTALLY THE PRIEST BECOMES CHRIST (AS OFFERER) AT THE CONSECRATION.

SACRAMENTALLY THE BREAD AND WINE BECOME CHRIST (AS VICTIM) AT THE CONSECRATION.

HUMAN PRIEST.... BREAD AND WINE

PRIEST TAKEN FROM AMONG US

GIFTS TAKEN FROM OUR LIVES

WE, THE PEOPLE

PRAY, BRETHREN, THAT MY SACRIFICE AND YOURS MAY BECOME ACCEPTABLE TO GOD THE FATHER ALMIGHTY.

THE PRIEST ASKS THE PEOPLE TO JOIN HIM IN OFFERING OUR SACRIFICE TO GOD.

NOTICE THAT THE PRIEST SAYS: <u>MY</u> SACRIFICE AND <u>YOURS</u>.

WE CAN BEST JOIN IN THE SPIRIT OF THE LAST THREE PRAYERS BEFORE THE CANON BY RECITING THIS PRAYER WITH THE ALTAR BOY AND REALLY MEANING WHAT WE SAY:

MAY THE LORD ACCEPT THE SACRIFICE FROM THY HANDS, TO THE PRAISE AND GLORY OF HIS NAME, FOR OUR ADVANTAGE AND FOR THAT OF ALL HIS HOLY CHURCH.

AMEN.

AT SOLEMN HIGH MASS THE PEOPLE ARE INCENSED HERE. YOU STAND.

HALLOW, WE PRAY THEE, LORD OUR GOD, BY OUR INVOCATION OF THY HOLY NAME, THIS SACRIFICIAL OFFERING, AND WORK UPON US UNTIL WE TOO BECOME AN ETERNAL OFFERING TO THEE. THROUGH OUR LORD JESUS CHRIST, THY SON, WHO LIVETH AND REIGNETH WITH THEE IN UNITY WITH THE HOLY GHOST, GOD, <u>FOR EVER AND EVER.</u>

AMEN.

THE SECRET PRAYERS ARE ONE OR MORE PRAYERS SAID BY THE PRIEST IN A QUIET VOICE. (THAT IS WHY THEY ARE CALLED SECRET.) THEY ARE SOMETHING LIKE THE COLLECTS AND CHANGE WITH THE FEAST.

THE LAST WORDS OF THE LAST SECRET PRAYER (HERE UNDERLINED) ARE SAID ALOUD.

KNOW YOUR MASS
CHAPTER EIGHT: THE HOLY OF HOLIES

NOW WE COME TO THE CENTER OF THE MASS, THE CANON (CALLED CANON, WHICH MEANS LAW, BECAUSE LIKE A LAW IT REMAINS UNCHANGEABLE).

WE CAN THINK OF THE PRAYERS OF THE CANON AS AN ALTAR FOR THE CONSECRATION, CONSISTING OF THREE PILLARS RESTING ON SIX STEPS. WE GO UP TO THE ALTAR ON ONE SIDE AND COME DOWN ON THE OTHER.

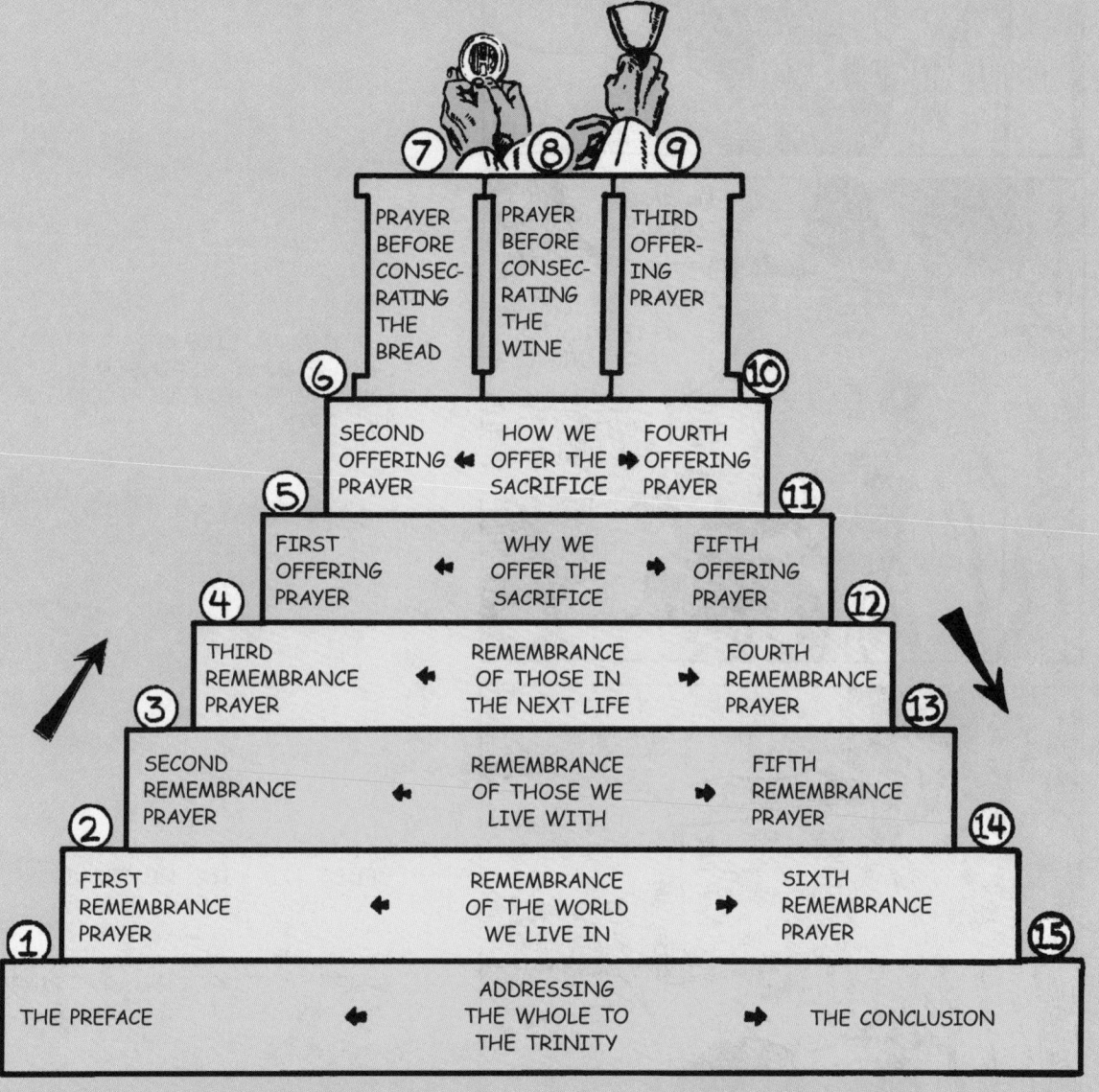

⑦ PRAYER BEFORE CONSECRATING THE BREAD	⑧ PRAYER BEFORE CONSECRATING THE WINE	⑨ THIRD OFFERING PRAYER
⑥ SECOND OFFERING PRAYER ←	HOW WE OFFER THE SACRIFICE →	FOURTH OFFERING PRAYER ⑩
⑤ FIRST OFFERING PRAYER ←	WHY WE OFFER THE SACRIFICE →	FIFTH OFFERING PRAYER ⑪
④ THIRD REMEMBRANCE PRAYER ←	REMEMBRANCE OF THOSE IN THE NEXT LIFE →	FOURTH REMEMBRANCE PRAYER ⑫
③ SECOND REMEMBRANCE PRAYER ←	REMEMBRANCE OF THOSE WE LIVE WITH →	FIFTH REMEMBRANCE PRAYER ⑬
② FIRST REMEMBRANCE PRAYER ←	REMEMBRANCE OF THE WORLD WE LIVE IN →	SIXTH REMEMBRANCE PRAYER ⑭
① THE PREFACE ←	ADDRESSING THE WHOLE TO THE TRINITY →	THE CONCLUSION ⑮

KEEP THIS DIAGRAM IN MIND AS WE GO THROUGH THE CANON. EACH PRAYER WILL BE NUMBERED TO CORRESPOND TO THE NUMBER IN THE DIAGRAM.

THE OFFERTORY ENDS AND THE CANON BEGINS AS THE PRIEST SAYS THE GREETING WHICH USUALLY INTRODUCES SOMETHING IMPORTANT.

THE CANON, LIKE OTHER PARTS OF THE MASS, BEGINS AND ENDS WITH A DEDICATION TO THE TRINITY.

THE PREFACE IS THE DEDICATION TO THE TRINITY AT THE BEGINNING OF THE CANON. IT IS ALSO A PRAYER OF THANKSGIVING. WE ARE GRATEFUL TO GOD FOR LETTING US TAKE PART IN THE MASS.

1. THE PRIEST READS THE PREFACE FROM THE MISSAL:

IT IS RIGHT INDEED AND JUST, PROPER AND HELPFUL UNTO SALVATION, ALWAYS AND EVERYWHERE TO GIVE THANKS TO THEE, HOLY LORD, FATHER ALMIGHTY, ETERNAL GOD, WHO WITH THINE ONLY-BEGOTTEN SON AND THE HOLY GHOST ART ONE GOD, ONE LORD; NOT IN THE ONENESS OF A SINGLE PERSON, BUT IN THE TRINITY OF A SINGLE NATURE. FOR WHAT WE BELIEVE FROM THY REVELATION CONCERNING THY GLORY, THE SAME WE BELIEVE OF THY SON, THE SAME OF THE HOLY GHOST, WITHOUT DIFFERENCE OR DISCRIMINATION. SO THAT IN CONFESSING THE TRUE AND EVERLASTING GODHEAD, WE SHALL ADORE DISTINCTION IN PERSONS, ONENESS IN BEING, AND EQUALITY IN MAJESTY. THIS THE ANGELS AND ARCHANGELS, THE CHERUBIM TOO, AND THE SERAPHIM DO PRAISE; DAY BY DAY THEY CEASE NOT TO CRY OUT, SAYING AS WITH ONE VOICE:

THE WORD EUCHARIST MEANS "GIVING THANKS." TAKING PART IN THE MASS AND RECEIVING HOLY COMMUNION IS ONE OF THE BEST WAYS TO THANK GOD FOR ANYTHING.

EACH OF US HAS A LOT TO THANK GOD FOR:

OUR PARENTS

OUR HOME

OUR COUNTRY

OUR SCHOOL

OUR FRIENDS

OUR CHURCH

THE MASS

> HOLY, HOLY, HOLY, LORD GOD OF HOSTS! HEAVEN AND EARTH ARE FILLED WITH THY GLORY. HOSANNA IN THE HIGHEST!

YOU KNEEL NOW.

THE SANCTUS (THE LATIN WORD FOR HOLY) IS THE PRAYER OF THE ANGELS ADORING GOD.

AS WE JOIN IN THIS PRAYER, THE ALTAR BOY RINGS THE BELL AND WE FALL ON OUR KNEES.

> BLESSED IS HE THAT COMES IN THE NAME OF THE LORD. HOSANNA IN THE HIGHEST!

WE ARE ENTERING THE HOLY OF HOLIES IN THE MASS.

2. THE PRIEST STARTS THE TE IGITUR:

"THEREFORE, MOST GRACIOUS FATHER, WE HUMBLY BEG OF THEE..."

IN THE TIME OF THE OLD TESTAMENT THE MOST SACRED PLACE IN THE TEMPLE WAS CALLED THE HOLY OF HOLIES. ONLY THE HIGH PRIEST COULD ENTER THIS ROOM.

THE ARK OF THE COVENANT WAS KEPT THERE.

KISSING THE ALTAR, HE SAYS:

"...THROUGH JESUS CHRIST, THY SON, OUR LORD..."

THE CANON IS EVEN MORE HOLY THAN THE HOLY OF HOLIES, YET GOD LETS ALL OF US TAKE PART IN IT.

"...TO DEEM ACCEPTABLE AND BLESS THESE GIFTS, THESE OFFERINGS, THESE HOLY AND UNSPOTTED OBLATIONS..."

THE PRIEST MAKES THE SIGN OF THE CROSS THREE TIMES OVER THE OFFERINGS AND ASKS GOD TO ACCEPT THE SACRIFICE TO BE OFFERED.

NOW, IN A QUIET VOICE, THE PRIEST SAYS THE FIRST OF THE REMEMBRANCE PRAYERS.

"...WHICH WE OFFER UNTO THEE IN THE FIRST INSTANCE FOR THY HOLY AND CATHOLIC CHURCH, THAT THOU WOULDST DEIGN TO GIVE HER PEACE AND PROTECTION, TO UNITE AND GUIDE HER THE WHOLE WORLD OVER; TOGETHER WITH THY SERVANT (BY NAME), OUR POPE, AND (BY NAME) OUR BISHOP, AND ALL TRUE BELIEVERS WHO CHERISH THE CATHOLIC AND APOSTOLIC CHURCH."

THERE ARE SIX OF THESE PRAYERS, THREE BEFORE THE CONSECRATION AND THREE AFTER IT.

IN THE FIRST REMEMBRANCE PRAYER THE CHURCH AND ALL ITS MEMBERS ARE BROUGHT INTO THE CANON.

3.

"BE MINDFUL, O LORD, OF THY SERVANTS AND HANDMAIDS..."

IN THE SECOND REMEMBRANCE PRAYER OUR FRIENDS, THOSE IN CHURCH, AND ALL WE WISH TO PRAY FOR, ARE REMEMBERED.

THE PRIEST PAUSES FOR A MOMENT AT THE BEGINNING OF THIS PRAYER TO INCLUDE ALL THOSE HE WANTS TO PRAY FOR.

DON'T FORGET TO MENTION THOSE YOU WANT TO PRAY FOR!

"...AND OF ALL HERE PRESENT, WHOSE FAITH IS KNOWN TO THEE, AND LIKEWISE THEIR DEVOTION, ON WHOSE BEHALF WE OFFER UNTO THEE, OR WHO THEMSELVES OFFER UNTO THEE, THIS SACRIFICE OF PRAISE FOR THEMSELVES AND ALL THEIR OWN, FOR THE GOOD OF THEIR SOULS, FOR THEIR HOPE OF SALVATION AND DELIVERANCE FROM ALL HARM, AND WHO PAY THEE HOMAGE WHICH THEY OWE THEE, ETERNAL GOD, LIVING AND TRUE."

MOM — DAD — SIS
BROTHER — PARISH PRIEST — TEACHER

4.

IN THE UNITY OF HOLY FELLOWSHIP WE OBSERVE THE MEMORY FIRST OF THE GLORIOUS AND EVER VIRGIN MARY, MOTHER OF OUR LORD AND GOD, JESUS CHRIST; NEXT, THAT OF THY BLESSED APOSTLES AND MARTYRS, PETER AND PAUL, ANDREW, JAMES, JOHN, THOMAS, JAMES, PHILIP, BARTHOLOMEW, MATTHEW, SIMON AND THADDEUS; OF LINUS, CLETUS, CLEMENT, SIXTUS, CORNELIUS, CYPRIAN, LAWRENCE, CHRYSOGONUS, JOHN AND PAUL, COSMAS AND DAMIAN, AND OF ALL THY SAINTS, BY WHOSE MERITS AND PRAYERS GRANT THAT WE MAY BE ALWAYS FORTIFIED BY THE HELP OF THY PROTECTION. THROUGH THE SAME CHRIST OUR LORD. AMEN.

5.

GRACIOUSLY ACCEPT, THEN, WE BESEECH THEE, O LORD, THIS SERVICE OF OUR WORSHIP AND THAT OF ALL THY HOUSEHOLD. PROVIDE THAT OUR DAYS BE SPENT IN THY PEACE, SAVE US FROM EVERLASTING DAMNATION, AND CAUSE US TO BE NUMBERED IN THE FLOCK THOU HAST CHOSEN. THROUGH CHRIST OUR LORD. AMEN.

IN THE THIRD REMEMBRANCE PRAYER THE GLORIOUS SAINTS IN HEAVEN ARE REMEMBERED.

WE MENTION BY NAME SOME OF THE FOLLOWING:

BLESSED VIRGIN MARY

SAINT JOHN AND SAINT PETER

OTHER APOSTLES

EARLY POPES

ROMAN MARTYRS

THERE ARE FIVE OFFERING PRAYERS IN THE CANON. TWO COME BEFORE THE CONSECRATION AND TWO AFTER IT. ONE, A SPECIAL ONE, IS SAID WITH THE PRAYERS OF CONSECRATION IMMEDIATELY AFTER THE ELEVATION OF THE CHALICE.

THE FIRST OFFERING PRAYER TELLS GOD THE REASONS FOR WHICH WE OFFER MASS.

6.

"DO THOU, O GOD, DEIGN TO BLESS WHAT WE OFFER AND MAKE IT APPROVED, EFFECTIVE, RIGHT, AND WHOLLY PLEASING IN EVERY WAY...

...THAT IT MAY BE FOR OUR GOOD, THE BODY...

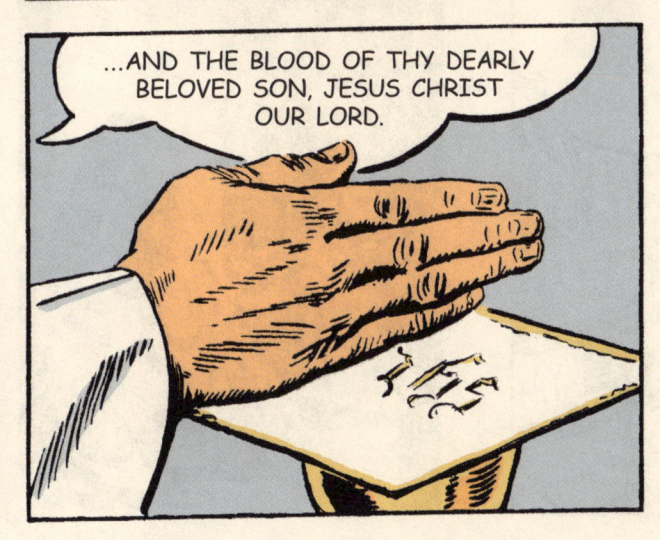

...AND THE BLOOD OF THY DEARLY BELOVED SON, JESUS CHRIST OUR LORD."

THE SECOND OFFERING PRAYER TELLS GOD HOW WE WISH TO OFFER OUR MASS.

DURING THE SECOND OFFERING PRAYER THE PRIEST BLESSES THE BREAD AND WINE THREE TIMES. THEN HE BLESSES EACH SEPARATELY.

NOW WE HAVE REACHED THE HIGHEST STEP OF THE CANON AND STAND BEFORE THE ALTAR OF CONSECRATION.

JESUS IS ABOUT TO COME DOWN UPON THE ALTAR.

THE BREAD AND WINE WILL BECOME TRULY HIS BODY AND BLOOD.

PAY VERY CLOSE ATTENTION.

IF A CIBORIUM OF HOSTS IS TO BE CONSECRATED FOR THE PEOPLE, THE PRIEST NOW UNCOVERS THE CIBORIUM. IN ONE ACT HE WILL CONSECRATE BOTH THE HOST IN HIS HANDS AND THE HOSTS IN THE CIBORIUM.

7.

WHO, THE DAY BEFORE HE SUFFERED,...

...TOOK BREAD INTO HIS HOLY AND VENERABLE HANDS...

...AND HAVING RAISED HIS EYES TO HEAVEN, UNTO THEE, O GOD, HIS FATHER ALMIGHTY...

AS THE PRIEST APPROACHES THE CONSECRATION, THINK WHAT IS GOING TO HAPPEN.

THE SUBSTANCE OF THE BREAD AND WINE IS GOING TO BE CHANGED INTO THE BODY AND BLOOD OF JESUS—BY THE POWER OF GOD WORKING THROUGH THE WORDS OF THE PRIEST.

THIS CHANGE OF SUBSTANCE FROM BREAD INTO CHRIST'S BODY IS CALLED TRANSUBSTANTIATION.

THIS IS CALLED A SUBSTANTIAL CHANGE BECAUSE THE SUBSTANCE CHANGES BUT NOT THE ACCIDENTS. THAT IS A SPECIAL WORD TO STUDY.

THE "ACCIDENTS" OF ANYTHING ARE WHAT WE FEEL, SEE, SMELL, AND TASTE.

THE SUBSTANCE IS WHAT SOMETHING REALLY IS IN ITSELF.

"...GIVING THANKS TO THEE..."

"...BLESSED, BROKE IT, AND GAVE IT TO HIS DISCIPLES, SAYING: TAKE YE ALL AND EAT OF THIS..."

"...FOR THIS IS MY BODY!"

BEFORE THE CONSECRATION

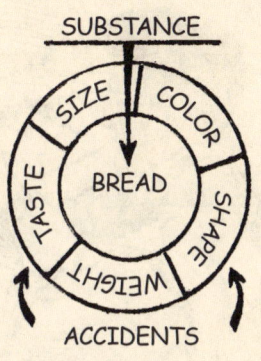

SUBSTANCE — BREAD
ACCIDENTS: SIZE, COLOR, SHAPE, WEIGHT, TASTE

YOU CAN SEE THE "ACCIDENTS" OF THE BREAD. BUT THE BREAD ITSELF —THE REAL SUBSTANCE—CANNOT BE SEEN OR TASTED EXCEPT THROUGH THE "ACCIDENTS" THAT APPEAR TO THE SENSES.

AT THE CONSECRATION THE ACCIDENTS OF THE BREAD AND WINE REMAIN, BUT THE SUBSTANCE CHANGES.

AFTER THE CONSECRATION

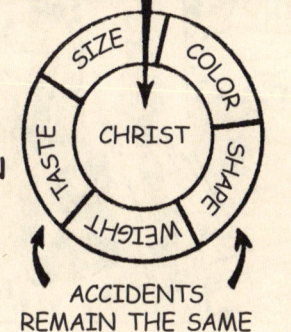

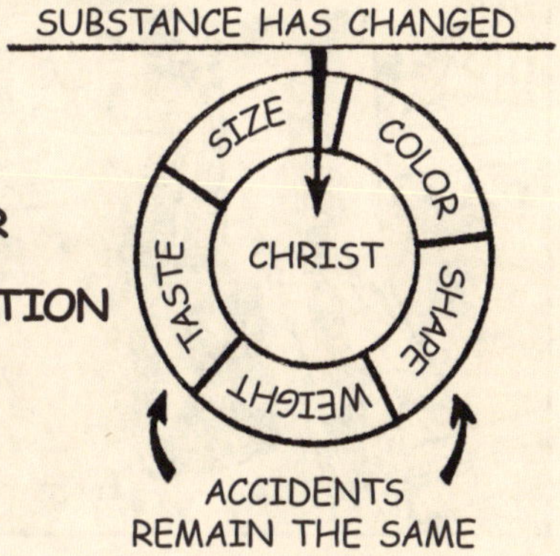

SUBSTANCE HAS CHANGED — CHRIST
ACCIDENTS REMAIN THE SAME: SIZE, COLOR, SHAPE, WEIGHT, TASTE

YOU CANNOT SEE THE CHANGE, BECAUSE ONLY THE SUBSTANCE WAS CHANGED—THE ACCIDENTS REMAIN THE SAME.

THE PRIEST NOW ACTS IN THE NAME OF CHRIST. SACRAMENTALLY HE IS CHRIST FOR THIS MOMENT. THAT IS WHY HE SAYS,

"THIS IS MY BODY."

THE PRIEST IMMEDIATELY BENDS HIS KNEE BEFORE CHRIST PRESENT IN HIS HANDS.

THEN HE RAISES THE BODY OF THE SON OF GOD FOR ALL OF US TO ADORE.

LOOK AT JESUS IN THE HOST AND WHISPER TO HIM: "MY LORD AND MY GOD!"

THOSE ARE THE WORDS THAT SAINT THOMAS USED WHEN JESUS APPEARED TO HIM AFTER THE RESURRECTION.

BUT THE CONSECRATION IS NOT YET OVER, FOR IN EVERY MASS THERE MUST BE A DOUBLE CONSECRATION.

8.

"IN LIKE MANNER..."

"...WHEN THE SUPPER WAS DONE,..."

"...TAKING ALSO THIS GOODLY CHALICE INTO HIS HOLY AND VENERABLE HANDS,..."

WHY MUST THERE BE A DOUBLE CONSECRATION IN EVERY MASS?

THERE MUST BE A DOUBLE CONSECRATION BECAUSE THE DOUBLE CONSECRATION RE-PRESENTS SACRAMENTALLY THE SACRIFICE OF CHRIST ON THE CROSS.

THE BLOODY SACRIFICE ON CALVARY

ON THE CROSS THE SACRIFICE WAS COMPLETED BY THE BLOOD BEING SEPARATED FROM THE BODY OF CHRIST IN A <u>PHYSICAL</u> WAY.

THE UNBLOODY SACRIFICE IN THE MASS

DOUBLE CONSECRATION

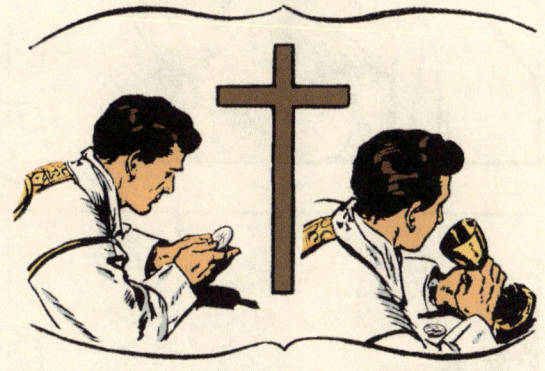

BREAD AND WINE ARE CONSECRATED SEPARATELY

IN THE MASS THE SACRIFICE IS COMPLETED BY THE BLOOD BEING SEPARATED FROM THE BODY OF CHRIST IN A SACRAMENTAL WAY.

...AGAIN GIVING THANKS TO THEE,...

SINCE OUR LORD IS GLORIOUS AND ALIVE IN HEAVEN, HIS BODY AND BLOOD ARE NO LONGER PHYSICALLY SEPARATED.

...HE BLESSED IT AND GAVE IT TO HIS DISCIPLES, SAYING: TAKE YE ALL, AND DRINK OF THIS:

FOR THIS IS THE CHALICE OF MY BLOOD, OF THE NEW AND ETERNAL COVENANT, THE MYSTERY OF FAITH, WHICH SHALL BE SHED FOR YOU AND FOR MANY UNTO THE FORGIVENESS OF SINS.

HE IS IN THE BLESSED SACRAMENT JUST AS HE IS IN HEAVEN, GLORIOUS AND ALIVE.

"AS OFTEN AS YOU SHALL DO THESE THINGS, IN MEMORY OF ME SHALL YOU DO THEM."

THEREFORE CHRIST IS PRESENT ENTIRELY—BODY AND BLOOD, SOUL AND DIVINITY—BOTH UNDER THE ACCIDENTS OF BREAD IN THE HOST AND UNDER THE ACCIDENTS OF WINE IN THE CHALICE.

THEREFORE IT IS ENOUGH TO RECEIVE CHRIST UNDER ONE SPECIES (FOR EXAMPLE, ONLY IN THE FORM OF BREAD). WE STILL RECEIVE THE WHOLE CHRIST.

ALTHOUGH THE DOUBLE CONSECRATION IS NECESSARY FOR THE UNBLOODY RENEWAL OF THE SACRIFICE OF CALVARY, ONLY ONE FORM OF THE EUCHARIST IS NECESSARY FOR HOLY COMMUNION.

WHEN THE PRIEST RAISES THE CHALICE FOR YOUR ADORATION, LOOK AT IT AND TELL JESUS HOW MUCH YOU LOVE HIM.

9. "MINDFUL, THEREFORE, O LORD, NOT ONLY OF THE BLESSED PASSION OF THE SAME CHRIST, THY SON, OUR LORD, BUT ALSO OF HIS RESURRECTION FROM THE DEAD, AND FINALLY HIS GLORIOUS ASCENSION INTO HEAVEN, WE THY MINISTERS, AS ALSO THY HOLY PEOPLE, OFFER UNTO THY SUPREME MAJESTY OF THY GIFTS BESTOWED UPON US..."

THE PRIEST NOW SAYS THE THIRD OFFERING PRAYER, THE SPECIAL ONE DIRECTLY CONNECTED WITH THE CONSECRATION.

IN THIS PRAYER ARE SUMMARIZED THE THREE GREAT IDEAS IN THE MASS:

1. REMEMBRANCE OF CHRIST.

"MINDFUL...OF THE BLESSED PASSION."

"...THE PURE VICTIM, THE HOLY VICTIM, THE ALL PERFECT VICTIM..."

2. SACRIFICE FOR SIN.

"THY HOLY PEOPLE OFFER... THE PURE VICTIM."

3. THE EUCHARISTIC FOOD.

"...THE HOLY BREAD OF LIFE ETERNAL..."

"THE HOLY BREAD OF LIFE."

...AND THE CHALICE OF UNENDING SALVATION.

THE FOURTH OFFERING PRAYER MATCHES THE SECOND OFFERING PRAYER (BEFORE THE CONSECRATION), FOR IT TELLS GOD HOW WE WISH THE MASS TO BE RECEIVED BY HIM.

ABEL'S SACRIFICE

10.

AND THIS DO THOU DEIGN TO REGARD WITH GRACIOUS AND KINDLY ATTENTION AND HOLD ACCEPTABLE, AS THOU DIDST DEIGN TO ACCEPT THE OFFERINGS OF ABEL, THY JUST SERVANT, AND THE SACRIFICE OF ABRAHAM OUR PATRIARCH, AND THAT WHICH THY CHIEF PRIEST MELCHISEDECH OFFERED UNTO THEE, A HOLY SACRIFICE OF THANKS AND A SPOTLESS VICTIM.

ABRAHAM'S SACRIFICE

MELCHISEDECH'S SACRIFICE

THE HEAVENLY FATHER IS ASKED TO ACCEPT OUR OFFERING JUST AS HE RECEIVED THE PLEASING SACRIFICES OF THE OLD TESTAMENT.

11.

"MOST HUMBLY WE IMPLORE THEE, ALMIGHTY GOD, BID THESE OUR MYSTIC OFFERINGS TO BE BROUGHT BY THE HANDS OF THY HOLY ANGEL UNTO THY ALTAR ABOVE, BEFORE THE FACE OF THY DIVINE MAJESTY,..."

THE FIFTH OFFERING PRAYER MATCHES THE FIRST OFFERING PRAYER (BEFORE THE CONSECRATION) FOR IT TELLS GOD THE REASONS FOR WHICH WE WANT HIM TO ACCEPT THE MASS...

THAT WE MAY BE FILLED WITH EVERY GRACE AND HEAVENLY BLESSING.

"...THAT THOSE OF US WHO, BY SHARING IN THE SACRIFICE OF THIS ALTAR,..."

"...SHALL RECEIVE THE MOST SACRED BODY..."

NOTICE HOW THE SIGN OF THE CROSS IS MADE FIRST OVER THE BODY AND BLOOD OF JESUS AND THEN ON THE PRIEST (WHO STANDS FOR US). SO WE ARE ALL UNITED WITH JESUS BY THE CROSS. AND THE GRACES AND BLESSINGS WE RECEIVE COME TO US BECAUSE WE ARE UNITED WITH JESUS.

"...AND BLOOD OF THY SON..."

NOTICE ALSO HOW MANY TIMES THE PRIEST MAKES THE SIGN OF THE CROSS. HE DOES THIS TO REMIND US AGAIN AND AGAIN THAT THE MASS IS THE RENEWAL OF THE SACRIFICE OF THE CROSS.

CHRIST'S BODY IS ON THE CROSS.

"...MAY BE FILLED..."

CHRIST'S BLOOD IS ON THE CROSS.

"...WITH EVERY GRACE..."

THE PRIEST AND WE ARE ON THE CROSS WITH CHRIST.

...AND HEAVENLY...

...BLESSING.

THROUGH THE SAME CHRIST OUR LORD. AMEN.

AS THE SIGN OF THE CROSS UNITES THE DIFFERENT PARTS OF THE MASS, SO THE DIFFERENT PARTS OF GOD'S KINGDOM ARE UNITED BY THE SACRIFICE OF THE CROSS. IN FACT, WE CAN PICTURE THE MASS AS A HUGE CROSS WITH ALL THE PARTS OF GOD'S KINGDOM JOINED TOGETHER BY JESUS.

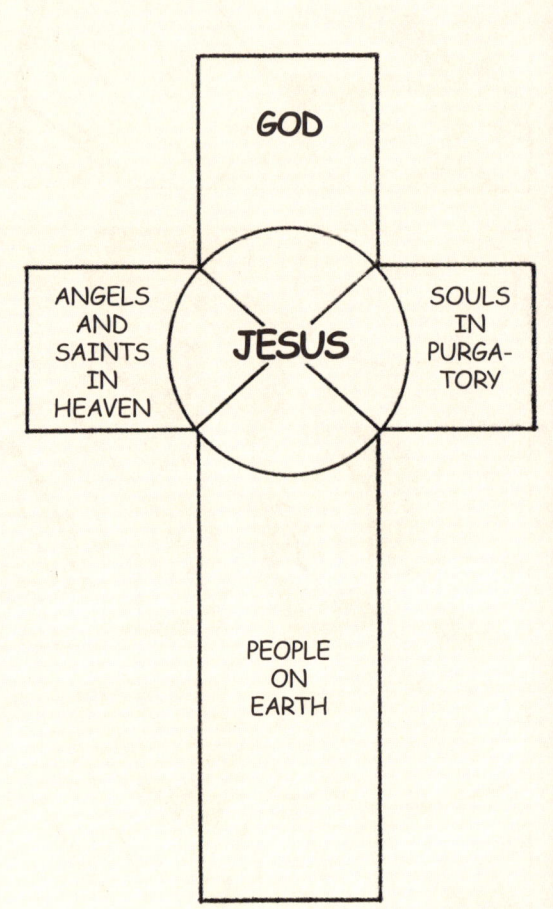

```
              GOD
              
ANGELS              SOULS
 AND                  IN
SAINTS    JESUS    PURGA-
  IN                 TORY
HEAVEN

            PEOPLE
              ON
            EARTH
```

12.

"BE MINDFUL, O LORD, ALSO OF THY SERVANTS AND HANDMAIDS WHO HAVE GONE BEFORE US WITH THE SIGN OF FAITH, AND REST IN THE SLEEP OF PEACE.

"TO THESE, O LORD, AND TO ALL WHO SLEEP IN CHRIST, WE BESEECH THEE TO GRANT, OF THY GOODNESS, A PLACE OF COMFORT, LIGHT, AND PEACE.

"THROUGH THE SAME CHRIST OUR LORD. AMEN."

NOW WE COME TO THE FOURTH REMEMBRANCE PRAYER. HERE WE REMEMBER ALL THOSE WHO ARE IN PURGATORY.

SOULS IN PURGATORY LOVE GOD, AND WANT TO BE WITH GOD. BUT THE MARKS OF THEIR SINS ARE STILL ON THEM, AND THEY HAVE TO BE PURIFIED BEFORE THEY CAN GO TO HEAVEN. IN PURGATORY THEY ARE WASHED BY SUFFERING—AND BY YOUR PRAYERS. THE MORE THEY ARE PRAYED FOR, THE LESS THEY WILL HAVE TO SUFFER.

13.

"TO US SINNERS ALSO,..."

THEN THERE IS A FIFTH REMEMBRANCE PRAYER. THIS ONE IS FOR OURSELVES, BECAUSE WE ARE SINNERS AND MUST PRAY FOR OURSELVES OFTEN.

WE WANT TO GET TO HEAVEN

"...STILL THY SERVANTS, TRUSTING IN THE GREATNESS OF THY MERCY, DEIGN TO GRANT SOME PART AND FELLOWSHIP WITH THY HOLY APOSTLES AND MARTYRS: WITH JOHN, STEPHEN, MATTHIAS, BARNABAS, IGNATIUS, ALEXANDER, MARCELLINUS, PETER, FELICITAS, PERPETUA, AGATHA, LUCY, AGNES, CECILIA, ANASTASIA, AND ALL THY SAINTS: INTO WHOSE COMPANY WE IMPLORE THEE TO ADMIT US, NOT WEIGHING OUR MERITS, BUT FREELY GRANTING US PARDON..."

SO WE PRAY VERY HARD TO PERSEVERE IN LOVING AND SERVING GOD.

FINALLY THERE IS THE SIXTH REMEMBRANCE PRAYER. IT IS VERY SHORT AND MERELY INCLUDES EVERYTHING ELSE THAT IS GOOD.

...THROUGH CHRIST OUR LORD.

14.

THROUGH WHOM, LORD, THOU DOST EVER CREATE, HALLOW, FILL WITH LIFE, BLESS,...

...AND BESTOW UPON US ALL GOOD THINGS.

THIS INCLUDES MATERIAL THINGS AS WELL AS SPIRITUAL.

THE PRIEST REMOVES THE PALL WHICH COVERS THE CHALICE, AND THEN HE MAKES A REVERENT GENUFLECTION.

15.

THROUGH HIM, AND WITH HIM, AND IN HIM...

THEN PICKING UP THE SACRED HOST THE PRIEST MAKES THREE SIGNS OF THE CROSS WITH IT OVER THE CHALICE, AND TWO BEFORE THE CHALICE.

...IS TO THEE, GOD THE FATHER ALMIGHTY IN THE UNITY OF THE HOLY GHOST...

THE PRAYER HE SAYS AS HE DOES THIS IS THE LAST PRAYER OF THE CANON. IT MATCHES THE PREFACE AND IS ALSO A PRAYER OF PRAISE IN HONOR OF THE TRINITY.

...ALL HONOR AND GLORY...

FINALLY THE PRIEST RAISES THE HOST AND CHALICE TOGETHER...

...OFFERING THEM TO GOD ONCE MORE...

...BUT OFFERING THEM TO US TOO...

...WORLD WITHOUT END.

AMEN.

FOR NOW WE ARE READY TO RECEIVE JESUS AS OUR BANQUET.

KNOW YOUR MASS
CHAPTER NINE: OUR BANQUET

AFTER THE CANON WE GO DOWN THE STEPS TO THE END OF THE MASS. (SEE THE DIAGRAM ON PAGE 34.) THESE STEPS ARE DIVIDED INTO TWO PARTS AS SHOWN BELOW.

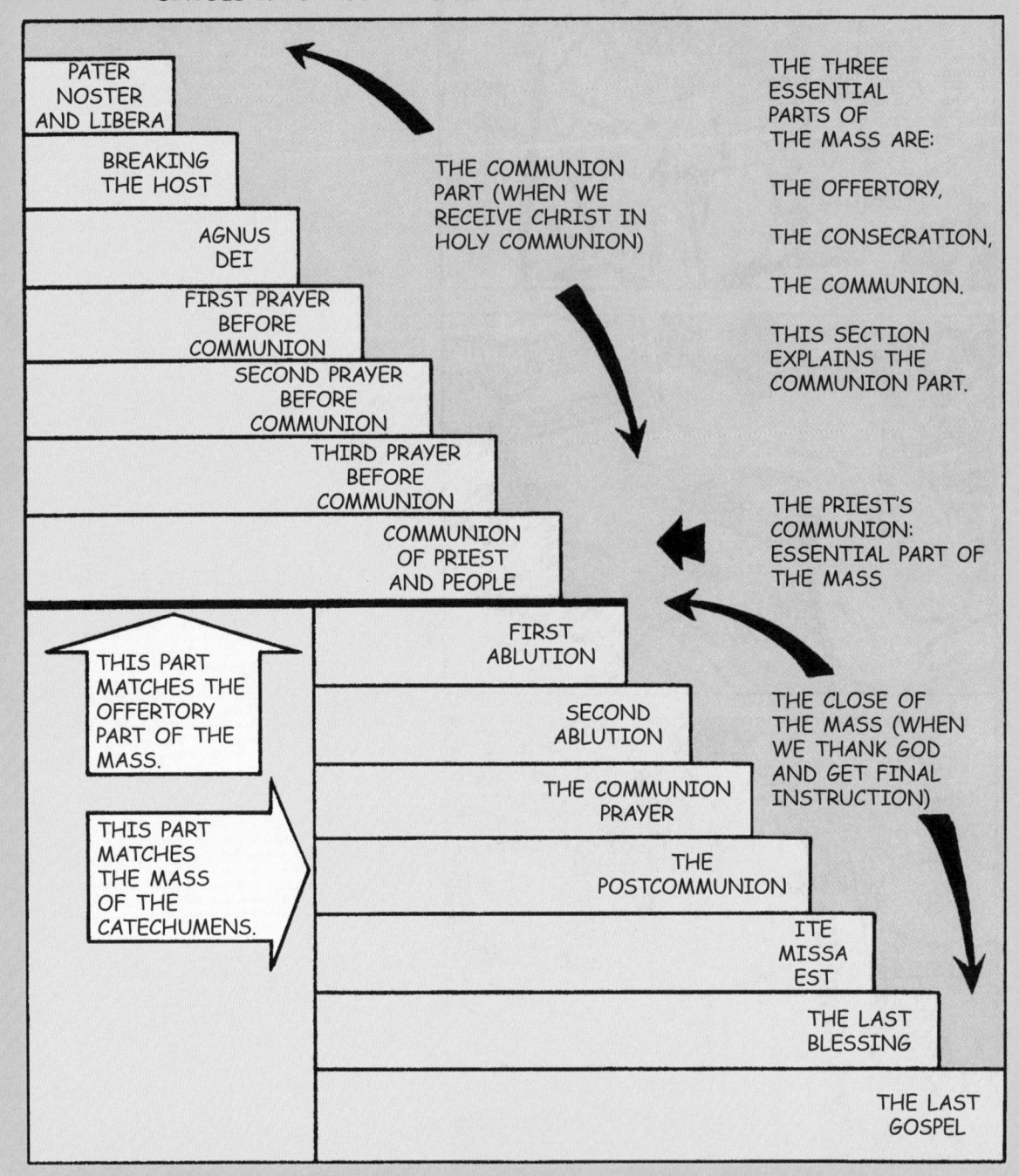

- PATER NOSTER AND LIBERA
- BREAKING THE HOST
- AGNUS DEI
- FIRST PRAYER BEFORE COMMUNION
- SECOND PRAYER BEFORE COMMUNION
- THIRD PRAYER BEFORE COMMUNION
- COMMUNION OF PRIEST AND PEOPLE
- FIRST ABLUTION
- SECOND ABLUTION
- THE COMMUNION PRAYER
- THE POSTCOMMUNION
- ITE MISSA EST
- THE LAST BLESSING
- THE LAST GOSPEL

THE COMMUNION PART (WHEN WE RECEIVE CHRIST IN HOLY COMMUNION)

THIS PART MATCHES THE OFFERTORY PART OF THE MASS.

THIS PART MATCHES THE MASS OF THE CATECHUMENS.

THE THREE ESSENTIAL PARTS OF THE MASS ARE:

THE OFFERTORY,

THE CONSECRATION,

THE COMMUNION.

THIS SECTION EXPLAINS THE COMMUNION PART.

THE PRIEST'S COMMUNION: ESSENTIAL PART OF THE MASS

THE CLOSE OF THE MASS (WHEN WE THANK GOD AND GET FINAL INSTRUCTION)

"LET US PRAY: DIRECTED BY SAVING PRECEPTS AND SCHOOLED IN DIVINE TEACHING, WE MAKE BOLD TO SAY:"

NOW WE BEGIN THE COMMUNION PART OF THE MASS. THIS IS THE BANQUET IN WHICH WE CAN RECEIVE THE BODY AND BLOOD OF JESUS CHRIST TO MAKE US STRONG SPIRITUALLY.

IN THE OFFERTORY PART OF THE MASS WE OFFERED JESUS TO GOD. IN THIS PART GOD OFFERS JESUS TO US.

WE START THE COMMUNION PART OF THE MASS BY SAYING THE BEST PRAYER WE KNOW...

THE LORD'S PRAYER

"OUR FATHER, WHO ART IN HEAVEN, HALLOWED BE THY NAME; THY KINGDOM COME; THY WILL BE DONE ON EARTH AS IT IS IN HEAVEN. GIVE US THIS DAY OUR DAILY BREAD; AND FORGIVE US OUR TRESPASSES AS WE FORGIVE THOSE WHO TRESPASS AGAINST US; AND LEAD US NOT INTO TEMPTATION,..."

IT IS THE BEST PRAYER BECAUSE IT IS THE PRAYER JESUS HIMSELF TAUGHT TO HIS DISCIPLES WHEN THEY ASKED HIM HOW TO PRAY.

NOTICE THAT WE ASK FOR "OUR DAILY BREAD." JESUS IN THE BLESSED SACRAMENT IS THE DAILY BREAD FOR OUR SOULS.

BE SURE TO SAY THE OUR FATHER WHEN THE PRIEST IS SAYING IT.

"...BUT DELIVER US FROM EVIL."

"AMEN."

NOW THE PRIEST TAKES UP THE PATEN, WHICH HAS BEEN LYING UNDER THE PURIFICATOR TO THE RIGHT OF THE CORPORAL. HE WIPES IT WITH THE PURIFICATOR.

AT THE END OF THE OUR FATHER WE ASK TO BE DELIVERED FROM EVIL. THE NEXT PRAYER TAKES THIS LAST IDEA AND DEVELOPS IT.

WE ASK GOD TO FREE US FROM:

PAST EVILS:	BAD HABITS
	OUR SINS

PRESENT EVILS:	TEMPTATIONS
	SICKNESSES
	EVIL COMPANIONS

EVILS TO COME:	MORTAL SINS
	INJURY
	DEATH

"DELIVER US, O LORD, WE BESEECH THEE, FROM ALL EVILS, PAST, PRESENT, AND TO COME; AND THROUGH THE INTERCESSION OF THE GLORIOUS AND BLESSED MARY EVER VIRGIN, MOTHER OF GOD, TOGETHER WITH THY BLESSED APOSTLES PETER AND PAUL, AND ANDREW, AND ALL THE SAINTS..."

WHILE SAYING THIS PRAYER THE PRIEST HOLDS THE PATEN ON WHICH THE HOST WAS OFFERED TO GOD AT THE OFFERTORY.
WE ASK GOD TO BE MINDFUL OF OUR GIFTS BEFORE WE ASK HIM FOR FURTHER FAVORS.

...GRANT OF THY GOODNESS...

...PEACE...

...IN OUR...

...DAYS...

THE PRIEST MAKES THE SIGN OF THE CROSS ON HIMSELF WITH THE PATEN.

THEN WE THINK OF THE HARM OF WAR...

...AND THE MISERY OF WORRY.

"...THAT, AIDED..."

"...BY THE RICHES OF THY MERCY, WE MAY BE ALWAYS FREE FROM SIN AND SAFE FROM ALL DISQUIET."

AND WE PRAY FOR PEACE IN THE WORLD AND IN OUR HEARTS.

IF THE EVIL OF SIN IS REMOVED, THERE WILL BE PEACE BOTH IN THE WORLD AND IN OUR HEARTS.

NOW THE PRIEST PLACES THE SACRED HOST ON THE PATEN.

THROUGH THE SAME JESUS CHRIST, THY SON, OUR LORD...

...WHO LIVETH AND REIGNETH WITH THEE IN THE UNITY OF THE HOLY GHOST, GOD...

...WORLD WITHOUT END.

AMEN.

TOWARD THE END OF THE PRAYER FOR DELIVERANCE FROM EVIL, THE PRIEST TAKES UP THE SACRED HOST AND CAREFULLY BREAKS IT INTO TWO PIECES.

THEN HE BREAKS A SMALL PIECE OFF ONE HALF WHILE PRAYING.

THERE ARE NOW THREE PIECES OF THE SACRED HOST ON THE ALTAR.

IS JESUS BROKEN INTO THREE PARTS?

NO, JESUS CANNOT BE DIVIDED. ONLY THE ACCIDENTS (WHAT WE CAN SEE) ARE BROKEN.

IN WHICH PART IS JESUS REALLY PRESENT?

JESUS IS REALLY PRESENT, WHOLLY AND ENTIRELY, IN EACH OF THE THREE PARTS.

DOES IT MEAN THAT THERE IS MORE THAN ONE JESUS?

NO, THERE IS ONLY ONE JESUS, BUT HE IS PRESENT IN THREE DIFFERENT PLACES.

THE PRIEST BREAKS THE HOST IN ORDER THAT HE MAY PUT A SMALL PIECE IN THE CHALICE.

THEN THE PRIEST SAYS ANOTHER SHORT PRAYER.

"MAY THE PEACE OF THE LORD BE ALWAYS WITH YOU."

"AND WITH THY SPIRIT."

"MAY THIS MINGLING AND HALLOWING OF THE BODY AND BLOOD OF OUR LORD JESUS CHRIST HELP US WHO RECEIVE IT UNTO LIFE EVERLASTING. AMEN."

AFTER MOVING THE SMALL PIECE OF THE SACRED HOST OVER THE CHALICE IN THE FORM OF A CROSS, THE PRIEST DROPS IT IN SO THAT THE BODY OF CHRIST UNDER THE FORM OF BREAD MINGLES WITH THE BLOOD OF CHRIST UNDER THE FORM OF WINE. THIS IS TO REMIND US THAT ALTHOUGH CHRIST'S BLOOD WAS SEPARATED FROM HIS BODY ON THE CROSS...

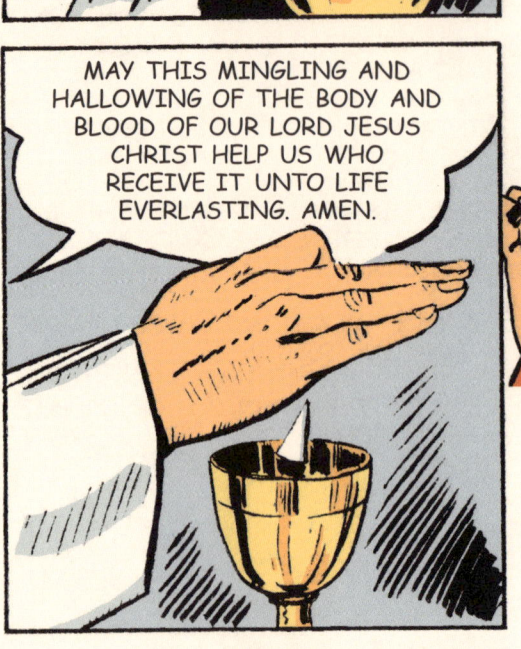

...BODY AND BLOOD WERE REUNITED ON EASTER SUNDAY WHEN CHRIST ROSE GLORIOUSLY ALIVE FROM THE DEAD.

"LAMB OF GOD, WHO TAKEST AWAY THE SINS OF THE WORLD, HAVE MERCY ON US."

"LAMB OF GOD, WHO TAKEST AWAY THE SINS OF THE WORLD, HAVE MERCY ON US."

"LAMB OF GOD, WHO TAKEST AWAY THE SINS OF THE WORLD, GRANT US PEACE."

THEN, STRIKING HIS BREAST AND CALLING ON CHRIST, THE PRIEST ONCE MORE BEGS FOR PEACE.

HE CALLS OUR LORD BY THE TITLE THAT SAINT JOHN THE BAPTIST GAVE TO JESUS WHEN HE SAW HIM BY THE BANKS OF THE JORDAN.

ISAIAS THE PROPHET AND SAINT JOHN THE EVANGELIST ALSO SPOKE OF JESUS AS THE LAMB. HENCE WE OFTEN SEE THE SYMBOL OF THE LAMB IN OUR CHURCHES.

(IN REQUIEM MASSES YOU WILL NOTE: INSTEAD OF PRAYING FOR PEACE FOR OURSELVES, WE ASK THE LAMB OF GOD TO GIVE THE SOULS IN PURGATORY ETERNAL REST.)

THE PRIEST NOW SAYS THREE SPECIAL PRAYERS IN PREPARATION FOR HIS RECEIVING HOLY COMMUNION.

THE FIRST OF THESE PRAYERS IS A PRAYER FOR PEACE, ESPECIALLY PEACE FOR THE CHURCH.

(THIS PRAYER IS OMITTED IN MASSES FOR THE DEAD.)

(IN A SOLEMN HIGH MASS THE KISS OF PEACE IS GIVEN AFTER THIS PRAYER TO SHOW THAT ALL WHO TAKE PART IN THE SACRIFICE ARE AT PEACE WITH ONE ANOTHER.)

PRIEST: O LORD JESUS CHRIST, WHO HAST SAID TO THY APOSTLES: PEACE I LEAVE WITH YOU, MY PEACE I GIVE TO YOU; REGARD NOT MY SINS, BUT THE FAITH OF THY CHURCH, AND DEIGN TO GIVE HER PEACE AND UNITY ACCORDING TO THY WILL. WHO LIVEST AND REIGNEST GOD WORLD WITHOUT END. AMEN.

LORD JESUS CHRIST, SON OF THE LIVING GOD, WHO BY THE WILL OF THE FATHER, WITH THE CO-OPERATION OF THE HOLY GHOST, HAST BY THY DEATH GIVEN LIFE TO THE WORLD, DELIVER ME BY THIS THY MOST SACRED BODY AND BLOOD FROM ALL MY SINS AND FROM EVERY EVIL. MAKE ME ALWAYS CLING TO THY COMMANDS, AND NEVER PERMIT ME TO BE SEPARATED FROM THEE. WHO WITH THE SAME GOD THE FATHER AND THE HOLY GHOST LIVEST AND REIGNEST GOD WORLD WITHOUT END. AMEN.

THE SECOND PRAYER BEFORE HOLY COMMUNION IS FOR UNION WITH JESUS. WE WANT TO STAY CLOSE TO HIM BY OBEYING HIS COMMANDMENTS.

LET NOT THE PARTAKING OF THY BODY, O LORD JESUS CHRIST, WHICH I, ALL UNWORTHY, MAKE BOLD TO RECEIVE, TURN TO MY JUDGMENT AND CONDEMNATION; BUT BY REASON OF THY LOVING KINDNESS, MAY IT BE TO ME A SAFEGUARD OF BOTH SOUL AND BODY, AND AN EFFECTIVE REMEDY. WHO WITH GOD THE FATHER, IN THE UNITY OF THE HOLY GHOST, LIVEST AND REIGNEST GOD WORLD WITHOUT END.
AMEN.

THE THIRD PRAYER IS TO BEG GOD TO HELP US MAKE A GOOD COMMUNION.

WHEN YOU RECEIVE HOLY COMMUNION BE SURE TO PREPARE BY ASKING GOD:

1. **TO BLESS THE CHURCH.**
2. **TO HELP YOU TO BE GOOD.**
3. **TO HELP YOU MAKE A GOOD COMMUNION.**

I WILL TAKE THE BREAD OF HEAVEN...

...AND CALL UPON THE NAME OF THE LORD.

JUST BEFORE HE RECEIVES HOLY COMMUNION THE PRIEST SAYS A VERY BEAUTIFUL PRAYER THREE TIMES. THE SERVER RINGS THE BELL.

YOU BOW SLIGHTLY AND STRIKE YOUR BREAST WITH YOUR RIGHT HAND.

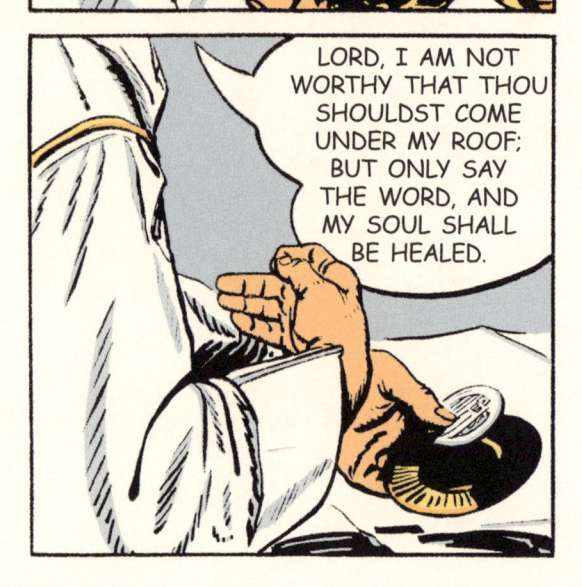

LORD, I AM NOT WORTHY THAT THOU SHOULDST COME UNDER MY ROOF; BUT ONLY SAY THE WORD, AND MY SOUL SHALL BE HEALED.

LORD, I AM NOT WORTHY THAT THOU SHOULDST COME UNDER MY ROOF; BUT ONLY SAY THE WORD, AND MY SOUL SHALL BE HEALED.

LORD, I AM NOT WORTHY THAT THOU SHOULDST COME UNDER MY ROOF; BUT ONLY SAY THE WORD, AND MY SOUL SHALL BE HEALED.

THIS PRAYER WAS FIRST SAID BY A ROMAN CENTURION.

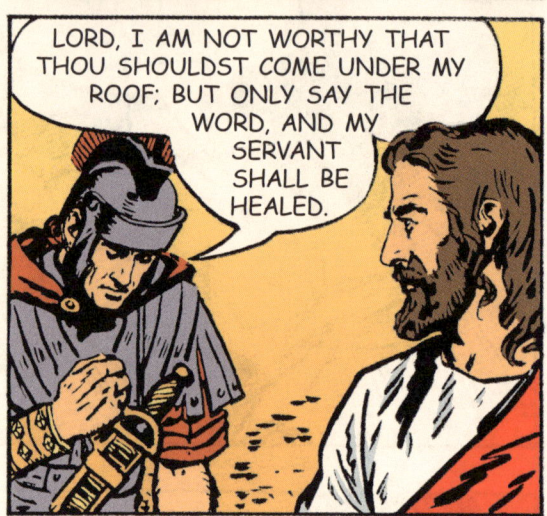

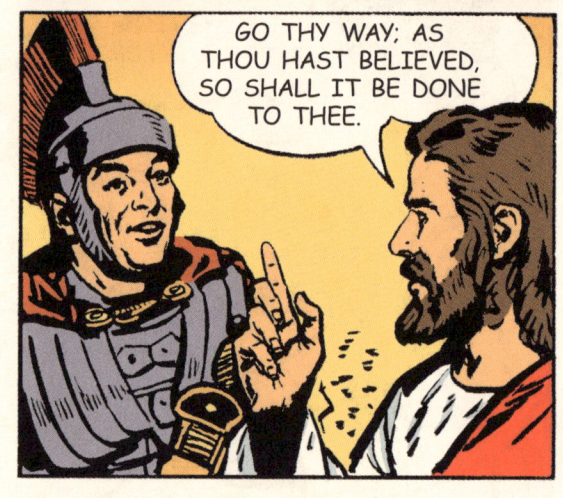

LORD, MY SERVANT IS LYING SICK IN THE HOUSE.

I WILL COME AND CURE HIM.

LORD, I AM NOT WORTHY THAT THOU SHOULDST COME UNDER MY ROOF; BUT ONLY SAY THE WORD, AND MY SERVANT SHALL BE HEALED.

GO THY WAY; AS THOU HAST BELIEVED, SO SHALL IT BE DONE TO THEE.

AND IN THAT HOUR THE SERVANT WAS CURED!

"MAY THE BODY OF OUR LORD JESUS CHRIST KEEP MY SOUL UNTO LIFE EVERLASTING. AMEN."

ALTHOUGH WE KNOW THAT WE ARE NOT WORTHY TO HAVE JESUS COME TO US, WE WANT HIM TO COME ANYWAY. AND JESUS COMES TO US IN HOLY COMMUNION BECAUSE HE LOVES US.

SO THE PRIEST RECEIVES JESUS UNDER THE FORM OF BREAD, AND HE STANDS SILENTLY FOR A MOMENT WHILE HE SWALLOWS THE HOST AND THINKS OF JESUS.

JUST AS FOOD BECOMES PART OF US WHEN WE EAT IT, SO WE BECOME UNITED WITH JESUS WHEN WE RECEIVE HIM IN HOLY COMMUNION.

"WHAT RETURN SHALL I MAKE TO THE LORD FOR ALL HE HATH GIVEN ME?"

WHAT SHALL WE GIVE JESUS FOR ALL HE GIVES US?
HE GIVES US HIMSELF. LET US GIVE HIM OURSELVES.

BOTH WHEN THE PRIEST RECEIVES JESUS UNDER THE FORM OF BREAD AND WHEN HE RECEIVES JESUS UNDER THE FORM OF WINE, HE PRAYS THAT THE HOLY EUCHARIST MAY KEEP HIS SOUL UNTO LIFE EVERLASTING.

THIS SAME PRAYER IS SAID WHEN THE PRIEST GIVES US HOLY COMMUNION.

THE PRIEST MOVES THE PATEN OVER THE CORPORAL TO PICK UP ANY CRUMBS THAT MAY REMAIN FROM THE SACRED HOST.

I WILL TAKE THE CHALICE OF SALVATION AND CALL UPON THE NAME OF THE LORD. PRAISING I WILL CALL UPON THE LORD, AND I SHALL BE SAVED FROM MY ENEMIES.

THE RECEIVING OF OUR LORD IN THE BLESSED SACRAMENT IS A PROMISE THAT WE SHALL RISE FROM THE DEAD AND LIVE FOREVER IN HEAVEN.

I AM THE BREAD OF LIFE. ...IF ANYONE EAT OF THIS BREAD HE SHALL LIVE FOREVER; AND THE BREAD I WILL GIVE IS MY FLESH FOR THE LIFE OF THE WORLD.

MAY THE BLOOD OF OUR LORD JESUS CHRIST KEEP MY SOUL UNTO LIFE EVERLASTING. AMEN.

HE WHO EATS MY FLESH AND DRINKS MY BLOOD HAS LIFE EVERLASTING, AND I WILL RAISE HIM UP ON THE LAST DAY.

HOW CAN THIS MAN GIVE US HIS FLESH TO EAT?

KNOW YOUR MASS — CHAPTER TEN

HOW TO RECEIVE HOLY COMMUNION

IF PEOPLE ARE GOING TO RECEIVE HOLY COMMUNION AT MASS, THEY MAY START FOR THE ALTAR RAIL AS SOON AS THE SERVER RINGS THE BELL RIGHT BEFORE THE PRIEST RECEIVES THE SACRED HOST.

IF MANY WANT TO RECEIVE, THEY SHOULD NOT ALL RUSH UP AT ONCE.

IF YOU ARE GOING TO RECEIVE...

...GO UP REVERENTLY WITH YOUR HANDS FOLDED.

TELL GOD YOU ARE SORRY FOR YOUR SINS WHILE THE SERVER SAYS THE CONFITEOR.

MAY ALMIGHTY GOD HAVE MERCY UPON YOU, FORGIVE YOU YOUR SINS, AND BRING YOU TO LIFE EVERLASTING.

AMEN.

Panel 1 (speech): MAY THE ALMIGHTY AND MERCIFUL GOD GRANT YOU PARDON, ABSOLUTION, AND FULL REMISSION OF YOUR SINS.

AMEN.

Bless yourself when the priest makes the sign of the cross.

Panel 2 (speech): BEHOLD THE LAMB OF GOD, BEHOLD HIM WHO TAKETH AWAY THE SINS OF THE WORLD.

Look at our Lord in the Host.

Panel 3 (speech): LORD, I AM NOT WORTHY THAT THOU SHOULDST COME UNDER MY ROOF; BUT ONLY SAY THE WORD, AND MY SOUL SHALL BE HEALED.

The priest says this prayer three times. Tell Jesus you want him to come to you.

WHEN THE PRIEST COMES TO YOU WITH HOLY COMMUNION:

1. OPEN YOUR MOUTH.
2. KEEP YOUR TONGUE OUT.
3. KEEP YOUR HEAD UP (DON'T BOW IT; DON'T PUT IT WAY BACK).
4. KNEEL STILL (LEAN AGAINST THE ALTAR RAIL).
5. DON'T PUT YOUR HANDS AGAINST YOUR CHIN (IF YOU ARE SMALL, PUT THEM BELOW THE ALTAR RAIL).
6. KEEP YOUR EYES DOWN (DON'T STARE UP AT THE PRIEST).
7. CLOSE YOUR MOUTH ONLY AFTER THE PRIEST HAS PUT THE HOST ON YOUR TONGUE (DON'T SNAP!).

THE RIGHT WAY

SOME WRONG WAYS

MAY THE BODY OF OUR LORD JESUS CHRIST KEEP YOUR SOUL UNTO LIFE EVERLASTING. AMEN.

AFTER RECEIVING HOLY COMMUNION:

1. RISE UP FROM THE ALTAR RAIL AFTER WELCOMING OUR LORD.

2. GO BACK TO YOUR PLACE REVERENTLY.

3. SWALLOW THE HOST AS SOON AS POSSIBLE.

4. BE SURE TO MAKE A REAL THANKSGIVING.

— TELL JESUS YOU ARE GLAD TO HAVE HIM AS YOUR GUEST.

— ASK HIM TO STAY WITH YOU ALWAYS.

KNOW YOUR MASS — CHAPTER ELEVEN

THANKS FOR THE BANQUET

"WHAT HAS PASSED OUR LIPS AS FOOD, O LORD, MAY WE POSSESS IN PURITY OF HEART, AND WHAT IS GIVEN US IN TIME, MAY IT BE OUR HEALING FOR ETERNITY."

YOU MAY SIT DOWN NOW.

THE PRAYERS IN THE MASS WHICH THANK GOD FOR COMING TO US IN HOLY COMMUNION ARE VERY SHORT. WE ARE EXPECTED TO STAY IN CHURCH AFTER MASS AND MAKE A PRIVATE THANKSGIVING WHENEVER WE CAN.

THERE ARE FOUR OFFICIAL PRAYERS OF THANKSGIVING IN THE MASS ITSELF.

THE FIRST TWO ARE SAID WHILE THE PRIEST WASHES OUT THE CHALICE.

FIRST THE PRIEST TAKES A LITTLE WINE INTO THE CHALICE AND DRINKS THAT TO REMOVE ANY DROPS OF THE PRECIOUS BLOOD WHICH MIGHT REMAIN. AS THE ALTAR BOY POURS THE WINE, THE PRIEST SAYS THE FIRST PRAYER.

"MAY THY BODY, O LORD, WHICH I HAVE EATEN, AND THY BLOOD WHICH I HAVE DRUNK, CLEAVE UNTO MY VERY SOUL; AND GRANT THAT NO TRACE OF SIN BE FOUND IN ME, WHOM THESE PURE AND HOLY MYSTERIES HAVE RENEWED. WHO LIVEST AND REIGNEST WORLD WITHOUT END. AMEN."

THEN THE PRIEST TAKES WINE AND WATER, LETTING THEM RUN OVER THE TIPS OF HIS FINGERS IN CASE ANYTHING FROM THE HOST IS ON HIS FINGERS. AS HE DOES THIS HE SAYS THE SECOND PRAYER.

THESE PRAYERS TELL YOU HOW TO PRAY AFTER COMMUNION:

1. ASK JESUS TO STAY WITH YOU.
2. ASK JESUS TO BLESS YOU.
3. ASK JESUS TO KEEP YOU FROM EVERY KIND OF SIN.

THE PRIEST WIPES HIS FINGERS AND THE CHALICE WITH THE PURIFICATOR.

THE PRIEST DRINKS THE ABLUTION.

HAVING WIPED OUT THE CHALICE AND COVERED IT, THE PRIEST GOES TO THE MISSAL TO READ THE THIRD AND FOURTH PRAYERS OF THANKSGIVING.

BOTH THESE PRAYERS CHANGE WITH THE FEAST.

THE FIRST IS KNOWN AS THE COMMUNION PRAYER. IT IS VERY SHORT AND REMINDS US OF THE OFFERTORY VERSE AT THE BEGINNING OF THE MASS OF THE FAITHFUL.

"WE BLESS THE GOD OF HEAVEN, AND BEFORE ALL LIVING WE WILL PRAISE HIM, BECAUSE HE HAS SHOWN HIS MERCY TO US."

THE COMMUNION PRAYER IS VERY OFTEN A VERSE FROM ONE OF THE PSALMS. IN THE EARLY YEARS OF THE CHURCH THE WHOLE PSALM USED TO BE SUNG AS THE PEOPLE WENT TO HOLY COMMUNION.

"THE LORD BE WITH YOU."

"AND WITH THY SPIRIT."

JESUS IS WITH YOU AFTER HOLY COMMUNION. YOUR HEART SHOULD BE SINGING. IF YOU ARE NOT REALLY HAPPY AFTER RECEIVING HOLY COMMUNION, IT IS BECAUSE YOU DO NOT THINK OF JESUS AFTER YOU RECEIVE HIM.

"MAY OUR RECEIVING OF THIS SACRAMENT, O LORD OUR GOD, AND THE PROFESSION OF OUR FAITH IN THE ETERNAL, HOLY TRINITY AND OF ITS UNDIVIDED UNITY BE OF PROFIT TO OUR HEALTH IN BODY AND SOUL. THROUGH OUR LORD JESUS CHRIST, THY SON, WHO LIVETH AND REIGNETH WITH THEE IN THE UNITY OF THE HOLY GHOST, GOD, WORLD WITHOUT END."

"AMEN."

THE FOURTH PRAYER OF THANKSGIVING AFTER COMMUNION IS CALLED THE POSTCOMMUNION.

SOMETIMES THIS IS A SINGLE PRAYER, SOMETIMES A SET OF PRAYERS. THE POSTCOMMUNION CORRESPONDS TO THE COLLECT AND THE SECRET.

BECAUSE THIS IS THE MOST IMPORTANT OF THE PRAYERS OF THANKSGIVING, THE PRIEST GREETS US BEFORE IT SO THAT WE SHALL PAY SPECIAL ATTENTION. THEN HE SAYS THE POSTCOMMUNIONS WITH HANDS EXTENDED JUST AS HE SAID THE COLLECTS.

THE POSTCOMMUNIONS ARE THE OFFICIAL PRAYERS OF THANKSGIVING FOR HOLY COMMUNION ON BEHALF OF THE WHOLE CHURCH.
THEY ARE ALWAYS ADDRESSED TO THE FATHER THROUGH THE SON IN UNION WITH THE HOLY SPIRIT.

(SOMETIMES THERE IS A SPECIAL LAST GOSPEL AND THE PRIEST HAS TO READ IT OUT OF THE MISSAL. WHEN THIS HAPPENS HE LEAVES THE BOOK OPEN AND THE ALTAR BOY KNOWS HE MUST BRING IT OVER TO THE GOSPEL SIDE OF THE ALTAR.)

KNOW YOUR MASS — CHAPTER TWELVE

LAST-MINUTE ORDERS

THE LORD BE WITH YOU.

AND WITH THY SPIRIT.

GO, YOU ARE SENT FORTH!

THANKS BE TO GOD.

MAY THE TRIBUTE OF MY WORSHIP BE PLEASING TO THEE, MOST HOLY TRINITY, AND GRANT THAT THE SACRIFICE WHICH I, ALL UNWORTHY, HAVE OFFERED IN THE PRESENCE OF THY MAJESTY, MAY BE ACCEPTABLE TO THEE, AND THROUGH THY MERCY OBTAIN FORGIVENESS FOR ME AND ALL FOR WHOM I HAVE OFFERED IT. THROUGH CHRIST OUR LORD. AMEN.

THE MAIN PART OF THE MASS IS OVER. WE HAVE OFFERED THE SACRIFICE AND RECEIVED HOLY COMMUNION. BUT BEFORE WE GO THE CHURCH WANTS US TO HAVE SOME LAST-MINUTE INSTRUCTIONS.

THE LAST PART OF THE MASS IS MADE UP OF THREE ACTIONS:

1. WE GET OUR ORDERS.
2. WE ARE BLESSED SO THAT WE WILL BE ABLE TO FILL OUR ORDERS.
3. WE ARE REMINDED OF WHAT GOD HAS TAUGHT US SO THAT WE SHALL KNOW HOW TO FULFILL OUR ORDERS.

← KNEEL DOWN NOW.

"MAY GOD ALMIGHTY BLESS YOU..."

"...THE FATHER, THE SON, AND THE HOLY GHOST."

"AMEN."

FIRST THE PRIEST TURNS TO THE PEOPLE AND SAYS: "GO, YOU ARE SENT FORTH."

WE HAVE BEEN UNITED WITH JESUS ON THE CROSS.
JESUS HAS COME TO US.
NOW WE MUST TAKE JESUS TO THE WORLD:
—BY WORKING HARD,
—BY BEING KIND TO OTHERS,
—BY GIVING GOOD EXAMPLE,
—BY DOING WHATEVER GOD WANTS US TO DO.

WE KNOW WHAT WE MUST DO. SO THAT WE SHALL HAVE THE STRENGTH TO DO IT, THE PRIEST GIVES US THE BLESSING OF THE CHURCH. SINCE THIS IS THE LAST BLESSING IN THE MASS IT IS CALLED THE LAST BLESSING.

"THE LORD BE WITH YOU."

"AND WITH THY SPIRIT."

BEFORE GIVING IT TO US THE PRIEST BOWS AND PRAYS TO THE HOLY TRINITY. HE REMINDS GOD OF THE SACRIFICE WE HAVE JUST OFFERED. THEN HE BLESSES US IN THE NAME OF THE TRINITY.

⬅ STAND FOR THE LAST GOSPEL

"THE BEGINNING..."

AFTER BLESSING US THE PRIEST DOES WHAT SEEMS TO BE A VERY STRANGE THING. HE GOES TO THE GOSPEL SIDE OF THE ALTAR AND READS THE LAST GOSPEL. SOMETIMES THIS IS A SPECIAL GOSPEL, BUT USUALLY IT IS THE SAME PASSAGE FROM THE VERY BEGINNING OF THE GOSPEL OF SAINT JOHN.

WHY DOES THE PRIEST DO THIS AT THE VERY END OF THE MASS?

HE DOES IT TO REMIND US OF THE INSTRUCTIONS WE RECEIVED IN THE MASS OF THE CATECHUMENS. IF WE ARE GOING TO BRING JESUS TO THE WORLD WE MUST REMEMBER THOSE INSTRUCTIONS.

"...OF THE HOLY GOSPEL..."

"...ACCORDING TO ST. JOHN."

"GLORY BE TO THEE, O LORD."

AGAIN WE SIGN OURSELVES WITH THE SIGN OF THE CROSS AS THE GOSPEL BEGINS.

WE ASK GOD TO BE IN OUR MIND AND HEART AND ON OUR LIPS.

WHEN WE GO OUT OF THE CHURCH TO WORK FOR GOD IN THE WORLD, WE MUST REMEMBER:

PRIEST: IN THE BEGINNING WAS THE WORD, AND THE WORD WAS WITH GOD, AND THE WORD WAS GOD. HE WAS IN THE BEGINNING WITH GOD. ALL THINGS WERE MADE THROUGH HIM, AND WITHOUT HIM WAS MADE NOTHING THAT HAS BEEN MADE. IN HIM WAS LIFE, AND THE LIFE WAS THE LIGHT OF MEN. AND THE LIGHT SHINES IN THE DARKNESS, AND THE DARKNESS GRASPED IT NOT. THERE WAS A MAN, ONE SENT FROM GOD, WHOSE NAME WAS JOHN. THIS MAN CAME AS A WITNESS, TO BEAR WITNESS CONCERNING THE LIGHT, THAT ALL MIGHT BELIEVE THROUGH HIM. HE WAS NOT HIMSELF THE LIGHT, BUT WAS TO BEAR WITNESS TO THE LIGHT. IT WAS THE TRUE LIGHT THAT ENLIGHTENS EVERY MAN WHO COMES INTO THE WORLD. HE WAS IN THE WORLD, AND THE WORLD WAS MADE BY HIM, AND THE WORLD KNEW HIM NOT. HE CAME UNTO HIS OWN, AND HIS OWN RECEIVED HIM NOT. BUT TO AS MANY AS RECEIVED HIM HE GAVE THE POWER OF BECOMING SONS OF GOD; TO THOSE WHO BELIEVE IN HIS NAME: WHO WERE BORN NOT OF BLOOD, NOR OF THE WILL OF THE FLESH, NOR THE WILL OF THE MAN, BUT OF GOD...

THAT THE WHOLE WORLD BELONGS TO GOD...THAT THE SON OF GOD BECAME MAN FOR US...

"...AND THE WORD WAS MADE FLESH, AND DWELT AMONG US..."

"...AND WE SAW HIS GLORY, GLORY AS OF THE ONLY-BEGOTTEN OF THE FATHER, FULL OF GRACE AND TRUTH."

"THANKS BE TO GOD."

THAT JESUS DIED TO SAVE ALL MEN FROM THEIR SINS...

THAT JESUS WILL ONE DAY COME IN GLORY TO GIVE LIFE EVERLASTING TO THOSE WHO LOVE HIM.